THE RIGHT

TO SELF-DETERMINATION
UNDER INTERNATIONAL LAW
AND POLITICS:
THE CASE OF THE BALOCH PEOPLE

HASSAN HAMDAM

Trafford
PUBLISHING

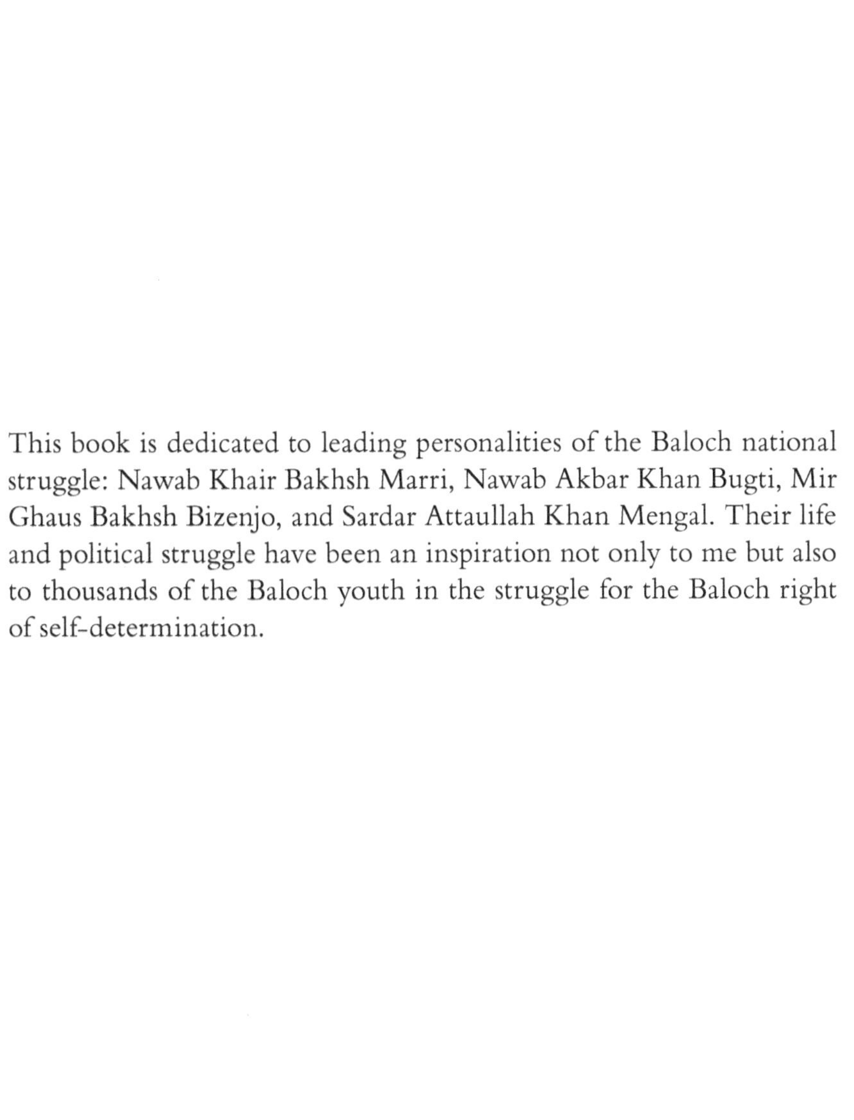

This book is dedicated to leading personalities of the Baloch national struggle: Nawab Khair Bakhsh Marri, Nawab Akbar Khan Bugti, Mir Ghaus Bakhsh Bizenjo, and Sardar Attaullah Khan Mengal. Their life and political struggle have been an inspiration not only to me but also to thousands of the Baloch youth in the struggle for the Baloch right of self-determination.

CONTENTS

FOREWORD

Hassan Hamdam's well-researched book *The Right to Self-Determination under International Law and Politics* is a welcome addition to the vast amount of literature on the subject. Its importance cannot be minimized, especially in the context of Balochistan national movement. It is the first book of its kind on this subject. The author tells me he compiled the material of the book for his PhD thesis, but due to personal reasons, he chose not to pursue the course.

A well-respected political and cultural activist, Hamdam is one of the leading members of the Baloch Human Rights Council, an advocacy organization based in London. I had a cursory glance at the contents of the book. Knowing the author well enough, I can say with confidence that he has done an excellent job in presenting Balochistan's case in the context of the right to national self-determination and freedom. This fundamental right to self-determination is enshrined in the United Nations Charter backed up by subsequent legal documents adopted by its General Assembly. In recent years, based on this principle, the UN supported the East Timorese and Kosovan peoples to successfully exercise their right to self-determination and independence. It even supported their armed struggles to defend themselves. Both Iran and Pakistan are signatories to the UN Charter, but aside from paying lip service, their actions point to the gross violations of this principle on a daily basis. In fact, the Pakistani and Iranian rulers are absolutely intolerant to those who dare to mention the word *rights*. Instead of accepting the reality, the rulers dub them traitors. To them, mentioning the UN Charter and the concept of self-determination is a capital crime.

Balochistan, as is well-known, was divided by the erstwhile British colonialists into three parts: the Eastern or Pakistani part, the Western or Iranian part, and the Northern or the Afghani part, which consists of the province of Nimroz and a sizable Baloch minority in the province of Helmand. The movement for political rights and self-determination is more advanced in Pakistani and Iranian parts, whereas in Afghanistan, there is a nascent movement that is more cultural than political. It must be mentioned here that these countries are multinational, but with the exception of Afghanistan, both Pakistan and Iran deny this fact. They both claim to be "Islamic nations." They forget that Islam is a religion, not a nation. Baloch people in both Pakistan and Iran have been denied basic human rights. Whenever the Baloch raise their voice, they are brutally suppressed. The great turning point came in 1974 when the Islamabad government launched a large-scale military operation in Balochistan at the behest of the Shah of Iran. They unconstitutionally dismissed the democratically elected provincial government of Sardar Ataullah Mengal, and all the Baloch leaders and hundreds of activists were put behind bars and tortured. Most of the weaponry, including helicopter gunships, were supplied by the Shah of Iran who feared a nationalist government on his eastern border. This collusion between Pakistan and Iran lasted for years. It is estimated that twenty thousand Baloch lives were lost during these bloody operations. The bitter irony is that after Ayub Khan, who was the first to impose a military solution on Balochistan, all the rulers who followed him—whether dictators or civilians when they first came to power, including the present prime minister—are on record that Baloch people had been unjustly treated. They promised that things would change and a new era of prosperity would be ushered in in Balochistan. However, these were all false promises. Things got worse with every power change. Once out of power, they would hypocritically apologize to the Baloch people.

In the past few years, the Pakistani rulers have introduced a new element of punishment in Balochistan. Whereas in the past they would arrest people, put them behind bars, and subject them to third degree torture without ever producing them before a court of law, now they simply make them "disappear" and torture them and then kill and dump their bodies at the outskirts of a village or town miles and miles away from their homes where no one will be able to recognize them. It is estimated that not less than five thousand activists and ordinary people—including doctors, engineers, writers, and journalists—have so far disappeared. This practice continues parallel with the ongoing military operations. Balochistan at present resembles a war zone. It has been totally militarized and resembles a ravaged occupied country.

Hamdam's book exposes the brutal policies, especially, of the Pakistani government. I therefore have no hesitation to recommend this book.

Akbar Barakzai
London, September 2020

ACKNOWLEDGMENTS

Many of my friends helped in one way or the other in the completion of this work. I would like to acknowledge the invaluable help of Dr. Naseer Dashti without whom it might have been impossible to complete this work. I am extremely grateful for his support and advice.

I would also like to express my gratitude to Ms. Hilary Rock, Samad Baloch, Qamber Malik, and Jamshid Amiri for their supports and encouragements.

LIST OF ABBREVIATIONS

AC	Atlantic Charter
ACHR	American Convention on Human Rights
ACHPR	African Charter on Human and Peoples' Right
AOK	Advisory Opinion on Kosovo
APODETI	Timorese Popular Democratic Association
ASDT	Timorese Social Democratic Association
AU	African Union
APOD	Timorese Popular Democratic Association
AL	Awami League
AN	Amnesty International
CSCE	Conference on Security and Cooperation in Europe
EC	European Community
EML	Eritrean Muslim League
EPLF	Eritrean People's Liberation Front
FRETILIN	Revolutionary Front for an Independent East Timor
FALINTIL	Armed Forces for the National Liberation of East Timor

HRW	Human Rights Watch
HRCP	Human Rights Commission of Pakistan
ICESC	International Covenant on Economic, Social and Cultural Rights
ICJ	International Court of Justice
ICCPR	International Covenant on Civil and Political Rights
IHRC	International Human Rights Covenant
INTERFET	United Nations Multinational International Force for East Timor
NATO	North Atlantic Treaty Organization
NAP	National Awami Party
OSCE	Organization for Security and Co-operation in Europe
OAU	Organization of African Unity
PCIJ	Permanent Court of International Justice
POLISARIO	Sahrawi Government in Exile or Liberation Movement
PPP	Pakistan People's Party
SADR	Sahrawi Arab Democratic Republic
SANU	Sudan African National Union
SSLM	Southern Sudan Liberation Movement
SPLA	Sudan People's Liberation Army
TWC	Third World Countries
UNGA	United Nations General Assembly
UDHR	Universal Declaration of Human Rights
UDT	Timorese Democratic Union
UG	Ustaman Gal
UDT	Timorese Democratic Union
UNAMET	United Nations Mission in East Timor
UNAMIS	United Nations Advance Mission in Sudan

C H A P T E R

ONE

INTRODUCTION

Two catastrophic wars in the twentieth century brought powerful empires down and paved the way for new emerging states on the map of the world. Experiencing the senseless destruction of wars, the leading nations realized that different ethnic groups and people would not accept the supremacy and abuse of others. Their interests and ambitions would be colliding with one another, and there would not be any peace and stability in the world unless there was an international force to maintain peace and security. First, the League of Nations was created in 1920, after World War I, to maintain world peace; but when the League of Nations failed to prevent the Second World War, then the United Nations was established in 1945 to harmonize nations and governments under international rules. Among the rules and principles for the smooth running of affairs of the larger community of nations, the right of self-determination was adopted as a legally binding international order of jus cogens (the compelling law) in the UN Charter. The responsibilities of states and the rights of people were defined, and the restraining measure of the state power was recognized. This international legal mechanism was

1

designed to work just like a modern state justice system, making sure that all people have access to a just legal institution and exercise their democratic rights around the globe. The international legal order was considered to be supreme, and all other rules of justice of the world would have to comply with the supreme command of international order.

Introduced during First World War as a political principle to resolve the emerging and complex national questions in Europe, the right of self-determination or freedom of choice without outside influence has become a legitimate right of the subjugated people in a twenty-first-century world. Intertwined with the theory of self-determination are secession, sovereignty, and territorial integrity, which have streamlined the debate in international legal circles in the last several decades. It is understood that self-determination has to be defined as a unanimous desire of people to choose their political status. The will of people is not only powerful but it also has the recognition and legitimate support of international legal norms. It is the will of people that makes a state legitimate, and it is also the desire of people that can challenge the rule of territorial integrity of the country they live in. The right to self-determination includes the right to independence and secession. There's no such thing as self-determination without a right of secession. The demand for political autonomy and freedom means respect for the will of people. Eight decades have passed since decolonization of the world began, and yet we are facing the same issues today.

From the beginning of the twentieth century, under various compulsions, the colonial powers reluctantly decided to begin a process of decolonization in Asia and Africa. They knew they were unable to continue their colonial ambitions, but at the same time, they wanted to safeguard their strategic and economic interests after they departed from those colonized regions. For that reason, they created many client states in different parts of the world. Their modus operandi was to divide nations and regions and carve a portion of a nation's land for their client state. In the process of these divisions, they separated numerous families, communities, and national entities in different countries. This has been causing political instability, ethnic tensions, internal conflicts, wars, and immense suffering for decades in those regions. These ethnic tensions in such so-called multinational states have never been genuinely addressed since the departure of colonial powers. Most of these countries are ruled by totalitarian regimes or one group of the population, excluding other groups from the power structure of the state. The inequality in the structure of power in multination states causes political unrest, and the situation intensifies when the state refuses to address and meet the demands of people. All such countries have failed to address the political issues and grievances of people. After years of suffering, people who were divided and incorporated in these artificially created countries are calling for recognition, justice, political autonomy, and the right to self-determination. The Baloch nation was among the unfortunate people who went through division of the former colonial nation and were incorporated in the newly created religious state of Pakistan in 1948.

With the beginning of the decolonization process in Africa and Asia during the 1950s, it became obvious that the world was in great need of some international leverage to maintain peace and security in the postcolonial era. After the adoption of the right of self-determination, it was necessary to couple it with other human rights conventions. Therefore, the principle of the right to self-determination was incorporated in various other international conventions and was taken under the wings of the United Nations. The right of self-determination became part of the International Human Rights Covenant (IHRC) of 1966, the International Covenant on Economic, Social and Cultural Rights (ICESC), and the International Covenant on Civil and Political Rights (ICCPR). The right of self-determination has also been recognized and defined in regional instruments as a principle of international law, such as in part 7 of the Helsinki Final Act (1975) of the Conference on Security and Cooperation in Europe (ACSCE) and in the African Charter on Human and Peoples' Right (ACHPR) in 1981.

The UN Declaration on the Granting of Independence to Colonial Countries and Peoples states that subjection, domination, and exploitation constitute a denial of fundamental human rights, are contrary to the Charter of the United Nations, and are an impediment to the promotion of world peace and cooperation. The United Nations General Assembly (UNGA) Resolution 2625 (1970) para 1 (3) adopted that no state would be allowed to oppress its citizens, as directed by article 1 (3) of the charter. This obligation is also included in para 5 and the 1966 International Covenant on Civil and Political Rights article 1 and the compliance provisions of articles 40 and 41. Following the UN declarations, the International Court of Justice (ICJ) also endorsed and defined the right of self-determination as the need to pay regard to the freely expressed will of people. The right to self-determination is considered to be the fundamental principle in the contemporary international law jus cogens, legally binding according to the Charter of the United Nations, which emerged from the Atlantic Charter (AC) on August 14, 1941. The UN Human Rights Committee has been urging all states to guarantee the human rights of people without any political hurdles. The states are advised to take positive action and respect human rights according to the Charter of the United Nations and international law. The international community is in complete agreement to provide international protection and more support to those people who desire to choose their political destiny.

The autonomy and right of self-determination constitute the most desirable wish of all human beings. The preservation of national identity and the desire to keep the national spirit alive are the driving forces behind every national struggle for freedom. The demand for a separate state has been changing the political map and environment of the world for centuries, and it seems that more changes are inevitable in the coming years. The right to self-determination has been declared as a human rights issue, and it can be realized through democratic values and international rules. The peaceful and legal method of self-determination carries the weight of international legal force and goes through the heart of human rights and dignity. A claim for democratic rights implies complete freedom to campaign for secession and a referendum on secession by the seceding nation, and the right to self-determination would exclusively lead it to independence. Nothing is conflicting or troublesome in valuing legitimate states on the one hand and accepting their division on the other. There is also nothing strange about redrawing existing state boundaries, as they were drawn by colonial powers without the consent of the people concerned. It may save lives and provide better security for the entire world.

As the right of self-determination has emerged from Western democracy, it has developed a strong political and legal base in those developed countries, but it is lagging in developing countries. The problem is that almost all developing countries are ruled by tyrants who have no desire to empower people or restrain their absolute power. In another word, they are ruled by oppressive and totalitarian regimes that refuse to accept international values and the democratic rights of people. They tend to destroy their country and people if it comes to power-sharing with their people. These kinds of behavior and denial of basic human rights have been causing unimaginable human loss and tragedy in different parts of the world for decades. The developing promotion and protection of human rights in the modern world is holding the hopes of subjugated and suffering people who continue their legitimate struggle for rights. However, since the Second World War, the world has seen many acts of genocide committed by tyrants around the globe. Countries like Bangladesh, East Timor, Eritrea, and South Sudan have achieved their freedom after sacrificing millions of lives. There are numerous ethnic groups— such as Kurds, Western Sahrawi, Tibetans, Sindhi, Baloch, and many others—who continue to struggle for the right to self-determination. Besides those nations, the Baloch national question in Iran and Pakistan is among the many unresolved issues of the colonial era that has been causing huge suffering, bloodshed, and regional instability since the incorporation of Balochistan into Pakistan in 1948.

Despite the recognition of the right of self-determination as a legal right of people in the international law, people are still denied their democratic rights, and millions have been suffering under cruel regimes in many parts of the world in our modern history. Some states have been ignoring international law for decades in the guise of sovereignty and territorial integrity without any consequences whatsoever. Even though the rule of state sovereignty does not give license to abuse the constitutional entitlements of people and their legal rights, neither does it allow the state to resort to unilateral threats or use force in dealing with the political demands for such rights. Besides the clear support of the United Nations, the recent rulings of the International Court of Justice also grant significant legal backing to the right of self-determination. This is the legal obligation of the international community to ensure that human rights cannot differ from country to country and are equally realized for all human beings according to international law and justice.

It has been observed throughout the known history of nations that whenever a certain group of people was ill-treated and suffered at the hands of a dominant group, they reacted with a strong sentiment of nationalism, demanding the right to self-determination. The modern world should deal with the right to self-determination according to its legally binding methods. For example, the claim of the Baloch people for the right to self-determination is a legal and democratic right under the international legal norms, and this right shouldn't differ from country to country. Like many other nations, the Baloch people should be allowed to decide their future by themselves, and the universal right of self-determination should be accessible equally to any people who wish to exercise it.

The human rights regime adopted by the international community through a legally binding framework has been increasing its efforts to meet the challenges it is facing. In recent decades, many decisions of the International Court of Justice have enhanced the international order of law and given hope to the subjugated groups and nations. Its decision displayed a concept of self-determination as a substantive right that accrues to peoples or non-self-governing territories, and those peoples or territories may wish to see it enforced. Its declaration on July 22, 2010, known as Advisory Opinion on Kosovo (AOK), paved the way for a peaceful settlement in such international disputes. This book is an effort to present the Baloch case for the right of self-determination in the context of UN human rights principles and the rulings and decisions of the International Court of Justice on various issues concerning the right of self-determination of subjugated nations.

To deal with the problems that emerged after the decolonization in Asia and Africa, the United Nations adopted the right of self-determination as a fundamental human right. The International Court of Justice made some historic decisions on the cases of subjugated nations in recent decades. Chapter 1 is the introduction that draws a general picture of the book on the political and legal dimensions of the right of self-determination.

The right to self-determination is one of the fundamental principles of the contemporary world, meaning it has been regarded as a rule of jus cogens in the norms of the United Nations. The concept aims to provide people with the right to freely decide their political destiny without external interference. The anti-colonial theory of self-determination empowers people to gain their independence and democratic rights from their oppressors. The two world wars ended with emerging liberation movements around the globe against colonial powers. The rights of people to govern their countries and the right of secession were recognized by the empires that became weak as the result of long-drawn-out wars. They reluctantly accepted emerging states on an equal footing with European people. Chapter 2 explores the history and the significance of self-determination.

In the contemporary world, the political ideology of nationalism became part of the national struggle against internal and external colonial methods. It is not just a simple part of international legal study but also an international doctrine that plays a crucial role in the law of self-determination. It also has its space in the international political and legal arena, and there is no doubt that nationalism has various political dimensions of its own that are the part and parcel of the nationalistic theory of a nation. The notion of nationalism had played a massive role in developing our modern world. It has been recognized by the universal force of the United Nations that, on one hand, reflects on the harmony of the world and, on the other hand, has a duty for the rights of peoples to promote the self-determination into the international order. Chapter 3 is a discussion on the history, definition, and context of nationalism in relation to the right of self-determination.

The principle of the right of self-determination is a human right–based rule that provides the condition in which people exercise their political, economic, cultural, and social rights. The right of all people to have the right of self-determination has been enshrined in the International Covenants on Human Rights. People have the fundamental right to freely decide their political status, which constitutes their internal and external positions in a country. It is the people's right to secede and establish their independent states if they wish to. The right of secession has been recognized as an integral part of international legal norms, especially in the case of tyranny and violation of internationally recognized human rights. This is to make sure that people shall have the power to challenge the unjust and illegitimate governments and states. Chapter 4 is a discussion on the human rights context of the right of self-determination and the role of the UN in cases of autonomy and issues of self-determination.

The notion of autonomy means the right of making one's laws or having the freedom of will and determination in certain matters. The concept is based on regional autonomy where a part of the country decides certain matters without the involvement of central government. The notion of autonomy is used in a different area of the government, and it ranges from local to international order.

In some cases, the autonomous area may take part in international decision-making and policy. Different forms of self-government have been defined, including cultural, territorial, and autonomy for minorities and indigenous people. Chapter 5 explores the meanings and numerous forms of autonomy, federation, sovereignty, and rights of minorities and indigenous people.

Autonomy is a pathway for spreading powers to a wider range of the country to keep the unity of the population. To avoid tension among various groups of people in a state, autonomy can be a better way than the use of force. Chapter 6 is a detailed discussion of various forms of autonomy and its relationship and comparison with the right of self-determination.

People in their different groupings and communities have created some form of rules and customs to manage their affairs for millennia, and various historical traces can be considered as the early form of law. International laws in the present shape evolved during the fifteenth and sixteenth centuries, navigating their way into the international legal order through the League of Nations and the United Nations. Chapter 6 is an exploration into sources of contemporary international laws regarding various conventions, treaties, and decisions of the International Court of Justice.

During the decolonization of the world from European powers in the 1950s, some regions and national entities were either amalgamated into new countries against the will of the people or left at the mercy of neighboring countries. For them, on the departure of Western powers, the colonial rules were replaced by stronger states in these regions. These nations were invaded again and faced even worse colonial measures than the former Western occupiers. However, in some cases, the international community came to their rescue and they got their freedom with the help of the United Nations—except for Bangladesh, which was able to obtain the ultimate support of India in the form of humanitarian intervention in 1971. The case of Western Sahara is still pending despite the resolution of the United Nations, the ruling of the International Court of Justice, and the official support of the African Union for a referendum. Chapter 7 is a discussion on the independent movements of East Timor, Eritrea, South Sudan, Western Sahara, and Bangladesh by exploring their tortuous journey to the right of self-determination.

The Baloch conflict with Pakistan and Iran is among the unresolved issues of the postcolonial world. Balochistan was occupied by the British in 1839 and later divided into many parts. After the British withdrawal from India, the Baloch state of Kalat declared its independence on June 11, 1947. However, the newly created religious state of Pakistan, with the help and agreement of the former colonial power, managed to annex it. Since then, the Baloch and Pakistan are engaged in a long-drawn-out bloody conflict. Chapter 8 is an account of the Baloch demand for the right of self-determination and its various aspects.

The concept of international humanitarian intervention is based on protecting people from being harmed by their states. The notion of international intervention outweighs the notion of state sovereignty, as it is to put an end to human rights violations and protect people from being harmed. Many actions of the religious fundamentalist states of Pakistan and Iran during the last few decades are in clear violation of international laws concerning the protection of the citizens. Chapter 9 is an analysis of the concept of international intervention in this context and is relevant concerning the continuous and blatant violations of the fundamental human rights of the Baloch people.

Chapter 10 contains concluding remarks.

THE HISTORY OF SELF-DETERMINATION

The right to self-determination is one of the fundamental principles of the contemporary world, meaning it has been regarded as a rule of jus cogens in the norms of the United Nations. The concept aims to provide people with the right to freely decide their political destiny without external interference. The political theory of self-determination evolved during the eighteenth century. During the early years of the twentieth century, Lenin and other socialist leaders, like Stalin, also advocated the people's right to self-determination. However, after adopting it as a strategy to end the colonial system by the League of Nations, it became a powerful tool for the suppressed nations. The concept was reenergized by United States president Woodrow Wilson in his statement for peace on January 8, 1918. After the Second World War, it paved the way for the Charter of the United Nations through the Atlantic Charter on August 14, 1941, and became one of the most important rules of international law.

The Political Origin of the Right to Self-Determination

The French Revolutionaries of the eighteenth century adopted the right of self-determination and promulgated the principle of centralizing it into the democratic rights of people throughout government institutions. It was much later during 1917 that the concept of self-determination was proclaimed by two internationally influential leading figures: Lenin and Wilson.

The leaders of the Soviet Union began to promote the right of self-determination before the Great Revolution of 1917. They enunciated that self-determination consists of three components. First, it could be involved by ethnic or national groups intent on deciding their destiny freely. Second, it was a rule to be adopted during the aftermath of military conflicts between states and for the allocation of territories to one or another power. Third, it was an anticolonial concept outlined to lead the liberation movements of all colonized countries. The first part of self-determination gave ethnic groups the right to decide their future freely; this includes all ethnic groups—not just those living under colonial rule. They are given the right to choose whether to secede or demand autonomy and stay a part of the larger structure. The concept was postulated by Lenin in 1916 in his conspicuous theses in which he asserted the necessity for political struggle and political democracy under self-determination. He expressed the theory even more in one of the articles he wrote to support a peace treaty with Germany, which was published in *Pravda* on February 21, 1918.

The Soviet Constitution granted the right to self-determination and accepted the Union Republic's right to secede. As Lenin was advocating for self-determination, he was also conceiving a Socialist Revolution unfolding throughout the world. Lenin's concept of self-determination was based on socialist political theory. He considered self-determination to be a revolutionary principle, and if necessary, the method of armed struggle could be used against existing states or colonial powers for gaining self-rule (Cassese 1995).

During the First World War, US president Woodrow Wilson was also brainstorming through the principle of the right of self-determination. Wilsonian self-determination was ploughing its way through the Western democratic philosophy of the "government must be based on the consent of the governed." For Wilson, self-determination meant the right of people who are free to choose their governments and political authorities. President Wilson's self-determination meant people having the right to decide their future with their own free will. He insisted that self-determination must be the key rule while dividing the Ottoman and Austro-Hungarian empires and redrawing a new map for new European territorial lines. Wilson pushed forward for the implementation of the principle in a nonviolent fashion through international organizations. He thought it was possible if the international community took real and tangible measures for its application, protecting minority and ethnic groups from oppressive states and regimes (Cassese 1995).

Cassese observed that since self-determination was particularized in the eighteenth century, the concept has been a vehicle for political issues and security of human rights. "It has been recognized as (i) a criterion to be used in the event of territorial changes of state; (ii) people should have right to choose freely their destiny through a plebiscite; (iii) an anti-colonialist postulate enjoy the right to secure their independent status with free will of populations; (iv) self-determination as a principle for freedom of a nation, an ethnic group in sovereign states. The principle led to the recognition of local governments like the Aland Islands which was based on the self-governing rule of democracy and rights of peoples. Despite the setback and failings of the League of Nations the case of Aland Islands was a benchmark for self-determination" (Cassese 1995, 32).

The principle of national self-determination was employed in the redivision of the former empires after the First World War. According to Mcwhinney (2007), the concept of political self-determination would emerge much later at the end of the Second World War. The self-determination of people in a sovereign state covers the internal self-determination of all people within the country's concern. The people have the right to elect their governments through a fair democratic process. The rights of linguistic minorities, ethnic groups, and indigenous populations must be equally respected through state institutions. Later, the right to choose was embodied in the Charter of the United Nations, in the International Covenant on Civil and Political Rights, and in the International Covenant on Economic, Social and Cultural Rights. Common article 1 paragraph 1 of these covenants provides that "All peoples have the right to self-determination. By that right, they freely determine their political status and freely pursue their economic, social, and cultural development" (Hannum 1990, 2). During the Second World War, the right of self-determination was made part of the Atlantic Charter of Franklin D. Roosevelt and Winston Churchill on August 14, 1941. By the end of the World War II, the leaders took the issue to the most significant San Francisco Conference of the spring in 1945, which had produced the United Nations Charter of 1945 and article 1 (2) of the UN "principle of equal rights and self-determination of peoples." The UN General Assembly resolution 1514 (XV) adopted the principle of right on December 14, 1960, by a vote of 89 to 0, expressing the equal rights and self-determination to all peoples and denouncing colonialism in all its forms. Declaring that the subjection of peoples to alien subjugation, domination, and exploitation constitutes a denial of fundamental human rights, is contrary to the Charter of the United Nations, and is an impediment to the promotion of world peace and cooperation (Mcwhinney 2007).

The aim was to empower people and nations in choosing their destiny by channelizing the assistance of the UN in the international arena. The notion of the UN in the terms of assessment was based on international law that holds the principles of the General Assembly recognized by nations in article (38) (1), the statute of the International Court of Justice. Despite the fact of the legal principle of self-determination, it is still lacking sufficient legal injunction from the UN and its member states. The biggest self-deceiving loopholes in the principle of self-determination are within the UN articles 2 (4) and 2 (7), barring the UN from intervening in the private matters of other states and considering that the domestic conflicts of any state are the business of the state concerned (Mcwhinney 2007, 4).

Advisory opinion of the International Court gave a clear dimension in holding South West Africa (Namibia) by an overwhelming majority. The UN General Assembly Resolution 2625 (XXV) of October 24, 1970, Declaration came up as a rule of the game concerning the friendly relationship among states and great powers competing in the Cold War to harmonize the peaceful means of existence among the nations. The peace and security policies were adopted during the Cold War and later periods, and diplomatic negotiation went on to ease the tension between the Soviet Union and the USA (Mcwhinney 2007, 5).

Self-determination in pre-UN times went through different forms in various contexts, ranging from national independence to the right to achieve a greater degree of autonomy in linguistic identity within a sovereign state. The UN Charter mentions self-determination twice, and it is enshrined in articles 1 (2) and 55 of the charter. Later, it was included in the International Covenants on Human Rights and in the Declaration on Friendly Relations, making it an integral part of human rights law, a fundamental right that has a universal application. Self-determination entered an important stage in its development in 1960 when the principle of self-determination evolved into the right of self-determination by the UN General Assembly in resolution 1514. Even through the Helsinki Final Act of 1975, the UN, ICJ, and international legal experts do not find any contradiction between the principles of self-determination and territorial integrity. The United Nations has failed to meet its responsibilities concerning self-determination and human rights protection around the globe.

Autonomy, self-government, right of self-determination, and *independence* are some words and political terminologies that have been used with some special meanings in the international arena to explain human groupings through the concept of self-determination or other relevant rights. These are also being used to point out that peoples maintain this right collectively as a group. The tendency behind this is that peoples want to be seen as a national group having a certain national feature.

The Significance of Self-Determination

Ethnic conflicts has been a popular term in our contemporary world for decades. In this context, analyzing the different dimensions of conflicts around the world is important. Today, such disputes are well documented throughout the international forum, and therefore it seems much easier to address them according to their base and roots. There are people like lawyers and politicians who advocate the terms *state* and *nation*, recognizing a governing body of a group of people over a piece of land, but it seems that they forget or avoid the core of the dispute, which is rooted in the most basic desire of human identity. These conflicts can be based on culture or language differences. Safeguarding smaller group interests against a more powerful one in a shared society creates differences among them. For instance, see the case of the Baloch people who has a different historical background, language, culture, and social behavior from the imported Pakistani language and culture. The other dimension is the powerful and the powerless. There is also a constant conflict between majority and minority or powerful and powerless groups. When these groups fight for their rights, there comes the demand for political autonomy.

The revitalization of ethnic conflicts in many post-1945 states—especially the call for identity and security of their language, culture, and autonomy—is still rife and ongoing in many countries around the globe. When one group is marginalized by a bigger group of people and deprived of equal rights and status, conflict is unavoidable. In some cases, even the democratic measures of equal rights may not be adequate, as free movement of the larger group causes the dilution of power through moving from the majority area into the traditional homeland of a minority group, which is exactly what is happening in Balochistan, not through the free movement of other ethnic groups but a preplan of Tehran and Islamabad. Whenever minority people in their multinational countries find that their ill-treatment and suffering in the hands of a larger group is continued and will follow more damaging consequences on their economy and social and cultural fabric, they shall react with a strong sentiment of nationalism, demanding the right to self-government. They may call systematic exploitation within a country as "internal colonialism" (Hannum 1990, 8–9).

The common understanding of ethnic tension is that it provides a political voice of dissatisfaction in the institution of a government hierarchy. The inequality in the structure of power in multination states causes political unrest. The situation is exacerbated when the state refuses to implement internationally recognized rules and human rights values. The failure of the state to accommodate the grievances of people would justify their demand for autonomy or a separate state according to international rules. The conflict between Pakistan and Balochistan has intensified throughout seventy years because of Pakistani refusal to recognize the democratic rights of Baloch people. The same behavior of the military establishment of Pakistan forced Bengalis to demand a separate state. Bengalis greatly contributed to the colonial efforts to create the artificial state of Pakistan on the map of the world, but when their rights were denied, they seceded from

Pakistan. Sindhis who were initially enthusiastic about the creation of Pakistan immediately felt that they were wrong and one colonial rule has been replaced by another. Unlike Bengalis, the Baloch were forced to join Pakistan; and after more than seven decades, Pakistan is still in a state of denial concerning the legitimate rights of the Baloch people. Therefore, the demand for self-determination and secession is inevitable.

State and nonstate actors express themselves as a nation or people not because these words are better understood in a public term, but rather, these nomenclatures are recognized as a form of certain international legal rules. Self-determination is one of the most important principles for human rights protection and yet the most compromised international rule in the name of so-called state sovereignty. Nevertheless, there is a legal framework in place to resolve international disputes; but unfortunately, there has never been a real attempt to develop a state's legitimacy concerning its human rights record, and neither there has been a great will for the implementation of international human values. Despite their state of ignorance, they blame the smaller groups as a source of division and trouble, which is completely contrary to the true nature of the conflict among them. Hannum (1990) observed that those who find minority groups to be manifesting disputes and conflicts overlook the great threats these groups face in their midst. Many conflicts in our modern world are international issues, as some ethnic groups have been divided into two or more countries—for example, Tamil, Kurds, Basque, Saamis, Baloch, and many others. When ethnic and national tension increases between opposing parties, their issues have to be handled through the international community by seeking a way out of a destructive conflict. The concept of sovereignty and self-determination goes hand in hand; therefore, a strong legal ground is needed to prevent abuse and promote human rights under international principles (Hannum 1990).

The development of the right of self-determination into international legal norms opened the doors of freedom for the colonized and oppressed nations around the globe. When decolonization began after the Second World War, the right of self-determination became the source of people's power to decide their political status, and it gave birth to many independent countries in many parts of the world. Throughout the process of decolonization, the United Nations has been playing a great role in granting the right of self-determination to many subjugated nations. However, many nations are still waiting for a determined effort by the international community in support of their endeavors to choose their political and economic destinies. The Baloch, Kurds, and Sindhis are glaring examples of people engaged in long-drawn-out conflicts with dominating powers in their respective regions.

CHAPTER THREE

NATIONALISM AND SELF-DETERMINATION

The earliest signs of nationalism can be traced back to ancient Sparta, Athens, and Rome. Later, the Greek and Roman ideology of nationalism was overshadowed by the barbaric and religious nationalist phenomena. The ideology diffused as a form of neo-nationalism in its early phase. During early modern times, the notion took various intellectual forms, navigating its way out of fascist and theologian nationalism to the modern doctrine of rights to exist as a nation or group alongside others in an equal manner. The political ideology of nationalism became part of the national struggle against the internal and external colonial methods. Thereby, people began to hear that all men are equal before the law or no people and nation shall be subjugated against their will. Nationalism is not just a simple part of the international legal study but also an international doctrine that plays a crucial role in the law of self-determination. It also has its space in the international political and legal arena, and there is no doubt that nationalism is a huge field in itself that goes right through the rationalistic theory of people as nations. The notion of nationalism had played a massive role in developing our modern world. The concept of nationalism has been recognized by the universal force of the United Nations that, on the one hand, reflects the harmony of the world and, on the other hand, lays down a duty for the rights of peoples to promote self-determination into the international order.

Nationalism

Nationalism is an essential part of life, and it seems impossible not to identify oneself with a nation or multination state. Generally, people believe that a state means a nation; but in reality, they are two different things. The expression of a state represents the notion of a politically independent area that is recognized by other states. One state may represent one ethnic group or nation or more than one group of people. For example, the United Kingdom is a state that represents four nations, and these nations are recognized as equal members of the union. On the other hand, a nation is a collective identity of a group of people who have evolved through their history, language, culture, and tradition.

A nation is born with a history of systematic living together generation after generation in a common territory, gaining a unique national characteristic that keeps a nation together to resist for its survival. For Stalin, a nation is a historically constituted stable community of people formed on the basis of a common language, territory, and economic and psychological makeup manifesting in common culture (Hutchinson and Smith 1994). Nationalism is the expression of love for one's community and group and is not used here as a prejudicial or xenophobic term. An extreme nationalist movement may harbor or display prejudices, but these kind of inclinations are not recognized as part of the doctrine of nationalism. Summers (2007) stressed that in many situations, nationalism is against xenophobic authority and powers. Nationalism is also not against the cosmopolitan system, but the demand for nationalism is acceptance of a national-based order besides the cosmopolitan one. Combining various definitions of nationalism, it can be said that it is the spirit of a nation that flows from the past through the present, aiming toward a future with a great desire for togetherness. Nationalism carries historical values, language, culture, and principles of ancestors. While sharing the glory, defeat, suffering, and sorrows of the past, nationalism binds together a community and attaches its past to hopes for the future. Gellner defined nationalism as primarily a political principle that holds the political and the national unit congruent. Nationalism as theory needs political legitimacy. Thus, for two men to be in the same nation, they require two things: (1) a common culture, understandings, and acknowledgment that the other is a fellow national and (2) the recognition of mutual rights and duties to each other in virtue of shared membership in it (Gellner 2006, 7).

Nationalism is also defined as the reflection of the ancient sense of distinctive human grouping based on the kinship of birth. It is also being defined as a recent development in modern history. The theory of nationalism did not only exist in the spirit of nations but also had a great role in shaping our modern world, navigating its way through the universal phenomenon of the international community. Modern nationalism emerged in the seventeenth century in Europe, Africa, and the Middle East. The concept of nationalism greatly influenced the revolutions in France and America in 1776 and 1789, which had shaken the old political hierarchies around the globe. During the French and American revolutions, nationalism gained political momentum throughout the world. The causes of that momentum may have varied in Africa, Europe, and Asia, but they resulted in a form of nationalistic moments in the spirit of being different nations. It defined people's political visions, determination, and political will to become a nation and handle their own matters. The ideology entered into the political dimensions of subjugated nations demanding autonomy and self-government and sovereignty. The doctrine became the voice of freedom struggle, and people demanded to be recognized as nations and have the right to self-government and to save their identity, language, and cultures without foreign interference in their business (Hutchinson and Smith 1994).

The notion of self-determination also applies to the problem of indigenous people, as both peoples and a nation have a right to self-determination according to international law. Indigenous people have been marginalized throughout modern history, forced into a nondominant position by later arrivals in their historical land. They are representing a mixed feature of indigenous people and the minority in their homelands. Indigenous people have a strong connection to their history and soil. They also have the right to a special status, autonomy, or self-determination (Gellner 2006).

It is understood that once a claim of self-determination has risen, it is highly likely that it will get stronger despite suppression and the onslaught of demanding people by various governments of the world. Why is it that a claim of self-determination is so often reached to a point where it becomes impossible to avoid violence and sometimes it becomes very difficult to deal with with peaceful means? The answer to that lies in the deeply rooted political history of the state concerned, and it also depends on the system of the troubled state. The majority of these conflicts are emerging from countries with no developed system and legitimacy of their governments. Many nationalistic movements are the results of the creation of artificial states after the Second World War. The intensity of the demand for the right of self-determination also results from the reaction of the state authorities. As observed by Mayall (2008), oppressive measures can be counterproductive and would confirm people's nationalistic sentiment regarding their struggle as a separate group of people. Lack of legitimacy, political will, and the ability to deal with these conflicts always lead to disaster. A state with a developed political system tends to provide political means for its disputes and political issues to be resolved according to internationally recognized rules.

Some of the states involved in national conflicts between various entities invalidly create some of their historical myths and theories to justify their claim of being a nation-state and defame those who do not agree with their artificial concept. The governments of these states use their school curriculum to draw a national picture that runs by a national spirit throughout state boundaries. The history of human grouping shows that this kind of artificial fixing of society would not last for long. As the theory of nationalism states very clearly, a state must be divided into nation-states, as the old map of the world still exists with its colonial lines and people will not accept these unjust solutions. People tend to go for their ethnic group and common sharing—for example, for their common land, language, myth of origin or ancestry, and a sense of a people with a shared history of triumphs and disasters that are also the deriving concept of a nation and run throughout its history. Historically, the world has been ruled by dynastic sovereign states. The inheritance of the rulers extended through war, coalition, or their marriages. The notion of sovereignty was considered to be related to the sovereign dynasty and their country. This theory of polity was changed by great French and American revolutions. Since then, the international political community has been based on the rule of national self-determination. The fall of the Roman, Habsburg, and Ottoman empires was a great blow to the traditional ruling concept. Thereby, the notion of a state as a family possession came to an end. The state became a nation-state, and the ownership was transferred to the population as people shared a society and the identity of a nation (Mayall 2008).

Ethnicity

Words such as *ethnic group* or *ethnicity* or *ethnic conflict* have become common terms in our modern world. An ethnic group is a community of people who share a long history of togetherness. The group bond lies under a collective notion of a people through its language, historical memories, culture, and custom. Ethnicity also can be distinguished by its specific characteristic of shared myth, homeland, ancestry, and a sense of solidarity among the group. There are tangible and intangible aspects of an ethnic group that play big roles in the formation of conflicts in our world. The concept of identity and uniqueness as a people is so important to them. This is the core of their political motivation and struggles to protect their common interest in a multinational state. However, it is not only the collective purpose of the group that seeks a political status. It is the dominant group that causes political pressure for a smaller group to use its identity for its survival or protect the interest of the nondominant group. *Ethnicity* is also used as a term of a nation or nationalism in the sense of their political and social construct. The ethnic group can be a huge or a small number of people, but in its uniqueness and features, such group remains the same (Weller and Wolff 2005).

Some of the social theorists, like Max Weber, believed that social phenomena such as ethnicity and nationalism would gradually decrease as industrialization and modernization push forward, but it seemed contrary to his prediction. During modern history, the political demands of ethnic groups grew dramatically around the world, asking for autonomy and recognition as such groups of people. These demands were largely made according to the rules of modern nations, but in some cases, they were ignored, which led to violence and catastrophic wars (Eriksen 1993). It is clearly understood that it is the wish of every ethnic group to preserve its rights to exist and fight back the threat of the dominant group. In the struggle for political recognition, the ethnic group may mobilize on nationalistic patterns in response to the exploitation of the dominant group. This is how a conflict of power begins in a multinational state. The ethnonationalism concept is designed to maintain and protect group rights through autonomy and power-sharing. It is important that the minority group's identity and language are protected. Giving a share in the power structure of the state is also important in dealing with ethnic discontent. In many cases, the political demands of minority groups are dealt with by assimilation, by suppression, and even worse, by ethnic cleansing and genocide. In these extreme cases, the government of the state and the dominant population manipulate all institutions of the state, which creates tension among the whole population. Therefore, the conflict intensifies between ethnic groups and state institutions, observed by Weller and Wolff (2005). These kinds of conflicts are mostly caused by the threat of marginalization, suppression, and denial of the political right of the smaller ethnic groups.

History shows that the threat of disintegration of a state gains momentum when an ethnic group of people is denied their constitutional rights. The politics of ethnicity, identity, and nationalism have been increasing around the world in terms of internal and external political struggle. Many nations or ethnic groups had to go through armed struggle and reached their destiny, and some of them had settled their demands through peaceful means. The ethnicity or nationalism became the source of the national struggle for identity and political rights during the 1950s. Alongside other groups, the indigenous population have also organized themselves and demanded their political rights over their respective regions, including Eskimos, Sami, Australian Aborigines, and Native Americans. Similarly, lots of ethnic groups have begun to struggle around the globe for their recognition and identity (Eriksen 1993).

Nationalism is a collective ideology of a group or nation to realize their political and social rights through a nationalistic struggle. The notion of ethnicity and nationalism gains momentum when a group or nation faces the oppressive policy of another group. The social and historical bond of the people keeps them together against a tyrannical government and an oppressive state. Their affection and loyalty toward the group is based on a survival mechanism that has evolved throughout history. The ethnicity, nationalism, and social bond are the fundamental structures of their identity as one group of people. Their distinctive feature of identity gives them the right to claim autonomy or self-determination under international law. Modern nationalism seems to be a reaction against the threat of political subjugation from a stronger group or state. For example, even if we exclude the historical background, the national struggle for the political rights of the Baloch people in Pakistan and Iran was triggered by the continuing authoritarian policies of these countries for many decades. When a state or regime refuses to accept the modern democratic value of international rules and uses draconian state measures against these groups, violent conflict would be inevitable.

SELF-DETERMINATION IN THE CONTEMPORARY WORLD

The right of all people to self-determination is one of the key principles of international law in the modern world. The rule is based on the democratic values of social, political, and economic rights, stating that people have the right to decide their political status. "By virtue of that right, they freely determine their political status and freely pursue their economic, social and cultural development." Thus, it is understood that all states have a responsibility to make sure that the internationally recognized rights of their people are respected and protected. There is an international obligation for states to provide a democratic environment where the principle of the right to self-determination is realized according to the international legal order. Any kind of obstruction of this legitimate international rule, particularly through force, would constitute a breach of the international order. The cardinal principle of self-determination is a human right issue, and it has been part of various international conventions since the end of World War II. The nationalistic political ideology of right to self-determination had gained momentum during the French and American revolutions. The notion was embraced by Lenin and the president of the United States Woodrow Wilson during the First World War, and it was considered to be essential for peace in the new emerging world. The right to self-determination was incorporated in the Atlantic Charter in 1941 and was ratified by the United Nations Charter in 1945.

After the First World War, the principle of self-determination was considered to be the international force against colonialism. One of the results of the devastating Second World War was the intensification of independence movements around the world, bringing with them various conflicts and disputes. Empires suddenly began to crumble, and the world needed a unifying force to deal with these issues. Therefore, the United Nations was created to meet these unfolding challenges. Soon it became the center of international politics and began to play its crucial role in the various parts of the world. The right of self-determination was adopted as part of human rights norms in the Charter of the United Nations, and people were given the right to choose their future by themselves. The sovereignty of states and the restrictions to their power were aligned with the new rules of international human rights and legal order.

The Role of the United Nations

The General Assembly of the United Nations had clarified the notion of self-determination in a wider context. It was mainly based on the values and the principle laid down by the French Revolution and the Declaration of Independence of the United States. Practically, it intended to proceed against colonial powers and become the voice of all occupied nations around the globe. It was further expressed in clear words in the resolution adopted in 1970, with the Declaration on Friendly Relations of the United Nations declaring, "By virtue of the principle of equal rights and self-determination of peoples enshrined in the Charter of United Nations all people have the right to freely determine their political status and pursue their economic, social and cultural development, and every state has the duty to respect this right." People were recognized as the holders of this right and self-determination as the core of these rights.

Self-determination became part of the Soviet Constitution when the Bolshevik party took over control of the vast multinational Russian Empire. Article 70 of the Soviet Constitution provided a "free self-determination of nations." According to article 72, each republic of the union enjoyed the right of secession from the USSR (Rudnitsky 1996, 73). This gave away a new shape to self-determination. It helped in the smooth transition of Central Asian Soviet republics from being parts of the union to independent states in the 1990s.

In the contemporary political milieu of the world, self-determination is considered to be one of the most essential and preconditional principles for peace and development. It is also considered to be the indispensable quick fix for the arising conflicts as states tend to refuse the legitimate rights of people. For the people who are still under the yoke of colonialism, the right of self-determination is the last standing remedy. Self-determination may give people the right to establish their sovereign state where an existing state completely failed to meet its obligation to protect and give a particular group of people equal rights. There are various nations without a state, and they rightfully deserve to have their separate state. There is consensus in the civilized world that the United Nations and the international community have a significant role to play in the world to keep peace and security. It has been stressed by people who are advocating for the total end of colonialism in all forms that all institutions under the United Nations have to function in the utmost form to reduce conflict and disputes in a world that is blinded by materialistic gain rather than human values and dignity. The demand for self-determination is extremely vital and needs a vigorous response from the United Nations to protect human rights and save people from great human suffering and loss. The groups who are struggling for their rights and identity must be acknowledged and protected through an international force. People have a strong sense of attachment among them and with their history, territory, culture, and language. They should be protected and allowed to exercise their right to choose their future.

However, the demand for self-determination must be approached logically. Rudnitsky (1996) opined that when dealing with a case of the right to self-determination, the following analyzing and evaluating must be made: (i) the need to find the real cause of the demands for self-determination and the disputes connecting them—for instance, the political, cultural, socioeconomic, and psychological environment and the historical background of the group; (ii) access to the population and information about such group and the posing problem and factors, including possible options for self-determination that would enable them to reach a meaningful solution of the conflict forever; (iii) the availability of appropriate democratic measure and systems essential for free expression of the will of the population concerned (Rudnitsky 1996, 80). Taking into account the bloodshed and genocide in various national liberation struggles and ethnic conflict, the duty of the United Nations and other actors involved in the self-determination issue must be focused on conflict prevention rather than postconflict reaction. Protective measures have to be taken to avoid violence, loss of human life, and eruption of other factors causing more complications to a peaceful settlement. The full force of the United Nations and other related international organizations dealing with a case of self-determination and human rights must be used to safeguard people from catastrophic wars. Effective interaction methods should be exercised through existing bodies like the High Commissioner for human rights–related issues anywhere in the world. There must be some special arrangement to indicate an early-warning mechanism to decrease the factors of violence and to balance the case of self-determination within internationally recognized legal norms. According to Rudnitsky (1996), such a monitoring system should be based on the following elements: (1) a thorough study of the real causes for the demand for self-determination; (2) the recognition and possible path of dealing with these causes and with a lurking perspective of a danger-related situation for internal and external means of solutions; (3) exploring the situation and conducting training and advisory assistance to relevant international institutions, including the United Nations; (4) pushing for vigorous diplomatic and nongovernmental efforts to reduce the potential sources of violence in the conflict. For this purpose, coordination between the United Nations and the regional actors should be utilized. (Rudnitsky 1996, 80).

Sovereignty and Statehood

The authority of a state and its jurisdiction has always been the most controversial matter in international politics concerning sovereign states. Because where there is sovereignty and freedom of a state to act and perform its affairs freely within and with other states, there are also some legal restrictions attached to that state of sovereignty. As observed by Hannum (1990), in actual meaning, there is no absolute sovereign state in the contemporary world. The undeniable fact is that the term *sovereignty*, from its introduction until today, had never been recognized as an international legal norm that all states agreed on. However, international legal experts believe that sovereignty is a practical concept to some extent in which all states make some particular decisions to restrain themselves from trespassing or going beyond their limits. But the suggested claim of state sovereignty in the sense of being above the international law is false. In practical terms and historical background, the terms *supreme power* or *sovereignty* may have been derived from an absolute spiritual leader or monarch who had supreme command and obedience to none. In a world where a large community of nations share responsibilities and power, the notion of the absolute power of a state is impossible. In the contemporary political milieu of the world, no state or power should be considered above international law. The equality of all states should lie in respect of internationally recognized standard rules.

Restriction on Sovereignty

In various situations, the state power is limited under universal rules. There are limitations on the protection of others, as a state is responsible for its action within or externally that may cause damage to another state and community. As soon as a state gains international recognition, it comes under great obligations based on internationally recognized principles. States response has been well-established for injuries to aliens and diplomatic immunity. The modern world doesn't accept the discriminatory treatment of foreign nationals and corporations. There are also restrictions on a state's power within its territory in dealing with its population. The fundamental rights of people have been developed as jus cogens under international legal norms. Human rights are protected under the umbrella of the United Nations, and crimes, such as genocide and systematic racial discrimination, against a group of people within a state carry severe punishments under the International Criminal Court. Human rights abuses are a great concern for international law.

Self-Determination and the State Sovereignty

The essence of the principle of self-determination of people was based on the right of people to choose their destiny. It was also to settle territorial questions in the interests of the people concerned. The Fourteen Points of President Wilson dealt with territorial settlements, embarking on new states out of the falling Austro-Hungarian and Ottoman empires.

The term *self-determination*, in its external and internal form, was considered to be the democratic right of people, meaning they are allowed to take matters into their own hands and not be ruled by others. The Wilsonian principles were intended to guarantee the right of minorities and those groups who identify themselves as a distinctive group of people with a certain character in the sense of their history, ethnicity, culture, tradition, and language. In the Paris Peace Conference of 1919, Wilson urged the League of Nations to recognize the right of self-determination of people. The Wilsonian draft stated that the agreeing powers who assure one another's independence and territorial integrity must remember that this agreement is subject to change in the future. As territorial changes could be required concerning self-determination, the principle of the political status of people must be respected by all states. The conference reflected on peace, on security, and also on the question of self-determination in the context of nationhood and rights of minorities and ethnic groups. The right to self-rule includes the right to separation from the oppressive nations, and the demands of any secession may meet through a democratically recognized referendum. There is no doubt that the success and failure of Wilson's plan was dependent on the support of the great powers. The great powers of the day had their interest attached for supporting or not recognizing a new emerging state on the map of the world. Hannum (1990) observed that in reality, self-determination in 1919 was more focused on the interest of stronger power rather than people. There were no plebiscites or appropriate referenda held for the people to decide their future; therefore, many nations were affected by the mapmaking of the great powers.

The collapse of the League of Nations and the emergence of the United Nations gave further impetus to the cause of the right of self-determination. In December 1960, the United Nations General Assembly declared that any nation and group can exercise the right of self-determination, and the notion was also supported by an international legal method. The declaration granted all power to territories and people to decide their future. The momentum was to bring freedom, peace, stability, and human rights and to stop all forms of colonialism in the world. The motion for independence was adopted, and the assertion was that the so-called inadequacy of political, economic, social, or educational preparedness should never serve to delay independence and freedom of people. The framework of decolonization began with the right to self-determination, and the principle became part of the international legal order of the world. The issue of settlers and minorities on a colonial territory was also dealt with by internationally recognized rules. Alongside other groups, the right to self-determination of indigenous people was also established.

UN General Assembly resolution 1541 adopted the guiding principle of self-determination and the obligation for its exercise. The resolution also made it clear in chapter 11 that a non-self-governing territory may emerge as a sovereign independent state or choose integration with an independent state. The demand and wish for independence normally navigates its way through the right of self-determination that is evident by the free will of people concerned. In the case of integration, the free will of people must be respected through a democratic process with full information and complete equal right between the people of the territory and the state they are amalgamating. However, there are no specific procedures and qualifications for a non-self-governing territory to rise as an independent state. Territories such as Belize and Western Sahara were recognized as separate states by the United Nations despite the claim of sovereign Guatemala over Belize and of Morocco and Mauritania over Western Sahara. Besides, the United Nations supported the notion of independence of Western Sahara by its resolution 1514 (XV) granting the right to the inhabitants to choose their future status.

The proclamation of Friendly Relations laid out the principle that "the emergence of a sovereign or independent state may choose integration or any other political status freely determined by a people constitute modes of implementing the right of self-determination by the people." This is recognized as a new standard of international relations between countries and international legal norms. Both international covenants on human rights established by the UN General Assembly in 1966 have article 1 in common, which states that all peoples have the right of self-determination. By that right, they freely determine their political status and freely pursue their economic, social, and cultural development. States are under obligation according to article 40 of the covenant on the issue of civil and political rights to report to the Human Rights Committee regularly regarding the implementation of the human rights safeguarded by the covenant. The right of self-determination is also adopted by the African Charter on Human and Peoples' Rights. Article 19 of the African Charter on human rights adopted a notion of equality and justice that states that "nothing shall justify the domination of a people by another." Article 20 sets the standard of self-determination in its three sub-articles that defined the right of self-determination, freedom, and support for the struggle to achieve its goal. Besides that, most of the countries around the world have accepted the right of self-determination through both covenants (Hannum 1990).

Autonomy is not a new term or political issue. It has been debated and practiced to some extent in the time of the post–Cold War. Many countries were reluctant to give autonomy in their jurisdictions and find the idea of a leading path to self-determination or secession. However, in the aftermath of the Cold War, the situation has changed completely in Central and Eastern Europe. The question of small nations and minorities emerged regarding the mechanism of their state and governments. The emergence of the Russian Federation and the independence of Georgia, Moldova, Armenia, Azerbaijan, and other Central Asian republics were changing the shape of the new world. The territorial integrity of states was outweighed by the will of the people of the region. The disintegration of Yugoslavia also proved that territorial integrity is not something that a state enjoys without the will of the people (Weller and Wolff 2005). The right to autonomy was reshaped and considered as a remedy to self-determination. It was no longer considered a dangerous path toward secession but a possible solution to meet the demand of people without endangering the boundaries of an existing state. In 1990, the Conference on Security and Cooperation in Europe (CSCE) started to promote and protect the ethnic, cultural, and linguistic identity of the different minorities in Europe and beyond. The conference has developed some meaningful approaches to achieve its aims. The organization was focused on the issues of minorities and their historical circumstances in the state concerned (Weller and Wolff 2005).

In 1991, the European Community (EC) advanced autonomy as an instrument for handling minority and ethnic conflicts. The community has established new means to recognize new emerging states in Eastern Europe from the dissolution of the Soviet Union and the disintegration of Czechoslovakia and Yugoslavia. The European Community considered that these were a small price for the future stability of the region. Autonomy has been adopted as a method for state-building before the above cases in Europe. This approach of devolution helped European states to maintain their territorial integrity and also made progress in people's lives through democratic means (Weller and Wolff 2005).

The United Nations has been advocating and pushing forward for autonomy for minority ethnic groups around the world. The major players of the United Nations have been persuading various regimes for giving away autonomy to ease the conflict of self-determination and secession in many parts of the world. The idea behind local and regional self-governance status may bring peace and stability to these countries. The theory of giving away autonomy as a state construction means that the movements for self-determination and ultimate secession may be avoided by this power-sharing method. One should not expect that autonomy per se would be sufficient to keep a dividing community together and bring an end to a separatist struggle. Autonomy should address the needs and the desires of people in the true constitutional sense and hold the balance of power between them. The administrative construction of the state must be designed to safeguard the identity of all people and generate a prospective success for the whole population.

Human Rights and Self-Determination

The principle of the right of self-determination is a human right–based rule that provides the condition in which people exercise their political, economic, cultural, and social rights. The right of all people to have the right of self-determination has been enshrined in International Covenants on Human Rights. The people have the fundamental right to freely decide their political status that constitutes their internal and external positions in a country. It is the people's right to secede and establish their independent states if they wish to. The right of secession has been recognized as an integral part of international legal norms, especially in the case of tyranny and violation of internationally recognized human rights. This is to make sure that people shall have the power to challenge unjust and illegitimate governments and states. The right of secession could be determined on the ground of ethnic characteristics and also based on group discrimination and violation of fundamental human rights.

Self-Determination and Conflict Resolution

The struggle for self-determination holds the hope of people for the recognition of their human rights and freedom. It provides an ideal theme for nationalist political forces to mobilize their people to pursue their cause of freedom. The self-determination struggles are mostly long-running armed conflicts between a state and a movement for self-determination and freedom. This kind of national liberation movement adopts various ways of warfare to sustain the struggle against a more powerful enemy for a long war. It is because of the nonintervention and unwillingness of international powers to bring both sides of conflict around a table and find a solution for the long and destructive wars. A conflict like self-determination will not cease by just ignorance of other actors. It makes the conflict violent, which destabilizes the country and the whole region. Weller and Metzger (2008) observed that the nature of self-determination claims is so powerful and has to be taken seriously by all members of the United Nations. The theory of self-determination has been derived from the unalienable human rights sources, making sure that all minorities and indigenous people benefit from the principle. The conventional way of dealing with issues of autonomy has been providing assistance to avoid a complete breakdown and secession—for example, the principle was used in the case of Åland Islands in Finland and South Tyrol in Italy. However, the situation has changed since the two Great Wars and during the Cold War up to 1988. It means that after the Cold War, there were new waves of demand for self-determination from the collapse of the Soviet Union and former Yugoslavia. Thereby, the international community became wholly involved in the conflict and had to enforce settlements.

National conflicts are not uniform or static. As the nature of international politics has changed, the conflicts—like self-determination—seem more cleared through internationally recognized legal and political norms bringing up a new way and methods to ease these conflicts Weller and Metzger (2008). There has been development in the field of settlements in the form of autonomy, which means a state may work out its problems without going through disintegration. The method may help to trade self-determination and cease the violence, but many governments find these settlements losing their grip on a region.

There is the universal realization that if self-determination of a conflict is not addressed on time, it will cause great destruction and destabilize the whole region. Therefore, it is a wise act to respond to the situation before it is too late and give the territory a special status within the country—for example, granting autonomy to the area and limiting interference of the central government. Sometimes there are insufficient and weak settlement actions taken by those involved to decrease the violence and tension between state and self-determination struggling forces. These kinds of poor agreements are taken because violence and war are a painful path for both sides. These agreements of power-sharing with a representative of minority ethnic group or ethnoterritorial entity pave the way for the transfer of more economic sources from the central government, and this can be sometimes guaranteed by international involvement. The decentralization of power to different authorities within the country makes it difficult to determine the sovereignty of a complete centralized phenomenon. The sovereignty of a state is no longer guaranteed in the new world of politics and international law. The sovereignty of a state lies in the treatment of its people, as people are the reason for its power, sovereignty, and the legality of its existence.

There are many good examples of settlements of conflict by granting autonomy. The decentralization of the power method was used in the Good Friday Agreement in 1998 with Northern Ireland. It was also the case in Bosnia and Herzegovina where central powers were shifted to the local level. It is generally believed that power-sharing works in some cases if it is done with goodwill and on time. However, in many cases of self-determination, such an approach may not be practicable; therefore the people have the right to decide their political status. Besides other political rights, some countries have accepted the right of self-determination in their constitutions, and people can choose between unions or break away from it without a war or hostility. The former Soviet Union, Ethiopia, Canada, and the United Kingdom are those countries that have adopted such constitutions. During the campaign of the Scottish referendum on September 18, 2014, the people of Scotland voted to stay with the United Kingdom.

It seems that modern international rules are clear about human rights and internationally recognized principles of human rights that would guarantee rights including economic, social, and political rights. The democratic nature of the right to self-determination is evident in that if people are given the right to decide their future, the issue of self-determination can be addressed and resolved without going through its destructive and painful phase of war and hostility. Despite having adequate international legal principles to deal with any international crisis, the world has failed to bring rogue states under its world legal order. It seems that the international methods of protecting people from being harmed still lack a tangible system of enforcement in international legal hierarchy. As long as rogue regimes find half-hearted attempts from powerful states and some loopholes in the international system of enforcement exist, they will not submit to international law.

CHAPTER FIVE

SWAY CONCEPT OF AUTONOMY

Autonomy is a special right given to those parts of the country where a population resides that differs from the other part of the state. The particular population may feel threaten or marginalized by the majority and, therefore, rightfully demand regional autonomy to protect their history, tradition, culture, and identity. The philosophy and concept of autonomy got importance with the development of morally responsible societies where the rights of people are respected. The notion of autonomy means the right of making one's laws or having the freedom of will and determination in certain matters. It is being used in different areas of governance and ranges from local to international order. The concept of autonomy can be better understood if it is compared with other power-sharing or diffusion-of-power arrangements. These methods are based on various political and constitutional changes—for example, the development of a federal system, decentralization, self-government, and self-determination. These systems differ from one another in a certain stage, as power-shifting takes place from one point to another through the different constitutional changes. The concept is based on regional autonomy where a part of the country decides certain matters without the involvement of the central government. In some cases, the autonomous area may take part in the international matter as well as in the national policymaking. Different forms of self-government have been defined—for instance, territorial and cultural for various groups, including minorities and indigenous people.

For philosophers like John Rawls, Robert P. Wolff, and Ronald Dworkin, autonomy is based on equality and justice. The Kantian concept of autonomy is free will and equal rights of people protected by an autonomous public justice system. James Crawford suggested that autonomous areas are regions of a state, usually possessing some ethnic or cultural distinctiveness, that have been granted separate powers of internal administration to whatever degree without being detached from the state of which they are part. Autonomy is based on constitutional power-sharing between states and different ethnic groups. These people should enjoy the legitimate right to keep their national and cultural identity. If a state denies such rights to the people concerned, they shall keep demanding them until the state grants them a certain status to guarantee and satisfy them. These guarantees may provide resolution of the conflict between majority and minority groups and improve their relationship with the state. Moreover, the organs of state transfer certain powers to the autonomous region and the regional institutions operate their authorities according to their own will. Sometimes, local decisions of the autonomous territory may differ from the institutional stand of the central government. The methods of autonomy agreement may be considerably different from case to case. The arrangement of autonomy goes from transferring legislative and judicial powers from the central organs to the regional authorities and a complete decentralization of powers and federalism (Heintze 1998).

Autonomy has been instrumental in many cases in Europe, Asia, the Middle East, and Africa. Examples can be cited in former Yugoslavia, Iraq, Ireland, Hong Kong, Puerto Rico, Eretria, Canada, and many other parts of the world. It has worked in some indigenous cases like Ålan Islands, South Tyrol, Kalaallit Nunaat (Greenland), and Puerto Rico. However, the practice of autonomy has also failed in many parts of the world, resulting in long bloody wars, destructions, and secession (Lapidoth 1997). As observed by Lapidoth, autonomy doesn't have an exact model or formula to be used for every single case, but there are useful rules, principles, and options for those who are seeking for an autonomous regime in their regions. Autonomy should be playing the main role in saving the rights of minorities and indigenous populations and those seeking self-determination. Moreover, it may be useful concerning other social, cultural, and economic issues (Lapidoth 1997).

Autonomy differs from the right to self-determination. The right of self-determination provides people with a right to freedom and to have their state. This is the principal part of international law to protect people and groups around the world and grant them the right to preserve their distinctiveness. On the other hand, the system of autonomy is instrumental to protect the right of minorities in the state they live in. Some scholars consider territorial autonomy as the opening pathway to self-determination. Because of the flexibility of the concept, it is widely used in states and international affairs. Self-government in a territorial body carries the notion of protection and promotion of the people concerned. Many other elements also may lead to autonomy— for example, a region geographically remote, the relationship of people to their homelands, especially their cultural and historical bond surviving throughout colonization of their region (Heintze 1998).

Experience shows that in cases where political rights were granted but did not meet the objectives of the minority group and the right of self-determination was not on the table, then autonomy was used to ease ethnic tensions. This approach was instrumental in easing various group conflicts for the last many decades that could have caused inconceivable destruction in the lives of people. It is believed that self-government and autonomy may bring different groups and minorities closer in a state. This decentralization of powers can open the doors for a positive society where the rights and equality of people and minorities would be protected through their self-government. Granting autonomy to reduce tension has been recognized by the international community as one of the good governing methods. When minority rights are addressed and protected by an institutional system, it gives a chance to various groups of people to live in peace instead of constant tension and wars (Heintze 1998).

According to Dworkin (1988), the rights of people must be respected at any cost, but it seems many governments treat their people differently as they join the powerful groups of people and rule others without any respect for their human rights.

The Essence of the Autonomy Notion

A country with different groups of people with various historical background is highly likely to face conflicts of power. Some states attempt to solve these issues of different people by force and assimilation, but others, especially with democratic valves, have been addressing these conflicts and empowering the people to decide their fate. One of these power-sharing measures is autonomy, which has been providing great service in many conflicts throughout the world. Although the awareness and the promotion of ethnic group rights arrived in Europe during the twentieth century, there has been little progress addressing these issues in developing the world. Thereby, the recognition demand of ethnic groups and indigenous populations is increasing around the world for their inalienable rights. As put forward by Lapidth (1997), the following human rights have to be addressed:

1. The right to equality and nondiscrimination
2. The right of the minority to preserve their culture, language, and religion
3. The right of indigenous populations to preserve their traditions and also have the right to their land and its natural resources
4. The right to self-determination

Delays in giving autonomy to concerned groups and ethnic entities give rise to conflicts of various intensities. There have been atrocities and violence for decades on those striving groups and nations around the globe dreaming to achieve their fundamental human rights and national identity. Many regions are still bleeding while the people there are facing a humanitarian crisis. Basques, Tamils, Kurds, Tibetians, Baloch, and Sindhis are examples of people suffering from no light at the end of the tunnel from the darkness of their situation. Various forms of autonomy may be desirable to these groups to achieve their goal and inspirations. However, it appears that the concept is not always meeting its goals for decreasing tension between battling groups, meaning that autonomy per se may not provide a solution for all expectations and wants of people. There are more dimensions and principles of international standards required to execute a long-lasting agreement that enables minority groups to preserve their identity. The principle of devolving power is based on public and community interests concerning avoiding a powerful centralization. In other words, the concept of autonomy has developed as a general international order to protect the rights of minorities and people in the political and economic arena. Spreading powers through democracy and allowing people to participate in their government affairs decrease the tension between majority and minorities (Heintze 1998).

Legality of Autonomy

The term *autonomy* is used in various legal perspectives in local or international legal order. Autonomy plays an important role in the governing system of a state, and according to international legal methods, autonomy means that a part of the state or a region runs certain matters without interference from central government. The notion is having the right to act independently in various matters through a constitutional framework by decentralization of power in a certain area of governing bodies of administration, legalization, and judicial system to the autonomous region. The autonomous area will be considered independent in decision-making and exercising the self-governing method in certain affairs (Heintze 1998). Autonomy has been recognized in international legal orders meaning freedom of action and policymaking in internal and, in some cases, international level. The matters of foreign policy, defence, and currency are usually run by central government. Internal matters concerning economy and culture may go to the autonomous entity.

The concept of autonomy is derived from the customary legal order, and it is increasingly helpful for the protection of minority rights. It is understood that the principle may provide minority groups with the right to preserve their identity from a majority ruling state. The concept grants minority groups a special status regarding governing their region, making their local laws, and enforcing them by their means. In 1991, the Badinter Arbitration Committee on Yugoslavia adopted autonomy as a specific right of minority people under the international legal law. The committee had suggested the Croatian autonomy has to be considered according to the international general norms, protecting the rights of the minority. The debate on autonomy has gained international momentum in the United Nations while deliberating on the protection of indigenous people. The draft

Declaration on the Rights of Indigenous Peoples article 31 states that these groups are entitled to autonomy or self-government. The declaration considers autonomy as a universal right of indigenous people that expands the principle into international law (Heintze 1998).

Autonomy, Minorities, and Indigenous people

The special rapporteur of the UN Sub-Commission Francesco Capotorti defined minorities as "a group numerically inferior to the rest of the population of a State, in a non-dominant position, whose members—being nationals of the State—possess ethnic and linguistic characteristics differing from those of the rest of the population." The United Nations Declaration on a minority was adopted in 1992 and not only defined a minority but also urged for their protection. Minorities Declaration article 1 states that "minorities as based on national or ethnic, cultural, and linguistic identity, and provides that states should protect their existence" (Capidoth 1997, 11).

Before World War I, there was no such mechanism or voice for minority protection. They suffered mass discrimination and injustice around the world. After the war, attempts were made to protect the rights of minorities. Their issues were addressed, and various protection measures were adopted in many new emerging states. As the territories of some countries increased, the League of Nations developed a new policy for minorities, and they were granted certain protections and autonomy in many countries. By the end of the Second World War, the minority rights protection campaign gained more momentum. It was obvious to the world that without some clear methods and rules, the rights of the minority or any other group shall not be protected. The International Covenant on Civil and Political Rights was established in 1966 to promote and protect ethnic minority rights from different actors. According to the civil and political rights of people, no group should be denied the right to practice their language, culture, and religion whether it is small or big (Lapidoth 1997).

During the Cold War, the political situation changed, bringing up new measures for the protection of human and group rights. Human rights protection advanced through a sequence of international meetings and conferences. The Copenhagen Meeting of the Conference on the Human Dimension of the CSCE in 1990 and the 1992 Helsinki decision of a High Commissioner on National Minorities navigated its way to the Organization for Security and Co-operation in Europe (OSCE) meeting in 1995 where national minority rights received international ratification. Articles 30, 32, and 33 of the documents asserted for the protection of national minority rights. The document suggested autonomy is one of the potential methods for solving ethnic conflicts. The recommendations were also made for "early warning" and "early action" to defuse the situation and make arrangements for meaningful negations. The issues of minorities have been widely debated during and after the Yugoslavian crisis. The structure of autonomy was drawn giving away the legislative, judicial, and executive power to the minority regions. New emerging states of Eastern Europe were recognized with conditions to guarantee the human and political rights of people and minority groups under international legal norms. According to the 1992 recommendations, Bosnia and Herzegovina were divided into various autonomous areas and minority rights were recognized constitutionally. This was not only to protect minority rights but also to accept the special status of their autonomous areas.

The methods and tactics of forced assimilation have been challenged by international laws. The rights of indigenous people are an international concern; therefore, protective measures have been adopted by the United Nations. In 1957, the convention for the protection of indigenous people stated that these people should enjoy special rights of autonomy or self-determination. Article 32 of the convention grants them the right to decide their citizenship concerning their custom and traditions. In 1991, the experts meeting in Greenland provided a path for the Human Rights Commission to safeguard the rights of the indigenous population around the world. The experts suggested that indigenous people have the right to self-determination and this right is inherent and fundamental to self-government. Besides, they have the right to equality, freedom, and human dignity and to exercise all human rights like other people (Lapidoth 1997).

Territorial Autonomy

There are various kinds of autonomy that are designed to balance the power of the state. However, territorial autonomy is the most important concept in terms of special territorial status. The construction of territorial autonomy comprises a complete self-governing system for the region that may deal with specific issues of minority groups and indigenous people—for example, the protection of their historical and cultural identity in their homeland. These agreements may meet through state and regional representatives. In some cases—for instance, Åland Island and South Tyrol—the arrangements were made through international organizations through internationally recognized legal methods (Heintze 1998).

In East Africa, Eritrea went under similar measures after Italy was defeated by Anglo-American forces in 1941, and the British attempt of dividing Eritrea between Ethiopia and Sudan failed. Thereby, the UN General Assembly passed a resolution according to the recommendations of the Commission for Eritrea in 1950 stating that Eritrea should be an autonomous region of Ethiopia. In 1952, Emperor Haile Selassie of Ethiopia ratified the act of federation accepting the autonomous status of Eritrea. Eritrea exercised administrative power by a chief executive who was elected by two-thirds of the Eritrean Assembly. The powers of the chief executive were like a head of state or governor who was responsible for enforcing the laws of the state. The Ethiopian emperor's representative in Eritrea had mainly ceremonial responsibilities in the region (Hannum 1990).

The involvement of the United Nations was somewhat similar to the Free City of Danzig and Memel. However, the situation of the City of Danzig differed from Eritrea, as it became an international city under the League of Nations. On the other hand, the Memel region went under Lithuanian sovereignty. The autonomous region of Memel exercised less power under the Lithuanian constitution than that of the Eritrean Federal Act that granted Eritrean territory much greater power to exercise freely in their regional matters. For example, it was the Lithuanian governor who appointed the chief executive officer of Memel, whereas the Eritrean chief executive was elected by the Eritrean Assembly. The aim in establishing an autonomous territory of Memel was to protect the rights of the German minority in the region, but in Eritrea, measures were taken to establish a politically autonomous territory under the notion of self-government. Apart from being dealt with by different measures and political arrangements, these regions shared the same concept of having more power and protection of their entities (Hannum 1990).

Autonomy is part of international legal obligations that differs from the right of self-determination in its degree of political policymaking. Generally, autonomy is considered to be the freedom of policymaking and action of a regional entity in its internal and local matters. The autonomous region also enjoys the power to make international agreements regarding cultural and economic issues or to join an international organization, although matters of foreign affairs, defence, and currency are usually held by the central government. For example, in Nordic countries, the Åland Islands became a member of the Nordic Council and Greenland terminated their European Community membership and Denmark is still a member of the EC. In some international decision-making, the central government consults with the autonomous region, as those decisions may have an impact on the particular region. To avoid disagreement and disputes, it will be wise and in the interest of both parties to define the rules of the game while establishing an autonomous regime. There are various powers to be divided into different areas. Some of the powers are only controlled by the central government, some of them are wholly transferred to the regional governing bodies, and some of them need joint actions. To exercise these powers without conflicts, there has to be good cooperation and consultations between the central government and the autonomous region. The representatives of autonomous areas exercise the granted powers on behalf of their population. The central government and the autonomous regional government jointly appoint the high-ranking officials. However, in some cases, the decisions of the autonomous population serve the public of the entire country, and this also works vice versa (Lapidoth 1997).

Establishment of autonomy may comprise international treaties through state constitution or a combination of all these instrumental measures. Changes in the status of an autonomous regime also require the involvement of these elements, and besides that, the most important role will include both parties, the regional and the central government of the country concern. Autonomy may include these actors:

It may have been developed through an international resolution of the United Nations—as Eritrean autonomy in 1952 that was adopted by the Ethiopian government after the resolution of the United Nations.

It may have been established by an international treaty—for example, the Paris Convention of 1924 regarding the Memel region or Convention of 1921 between concerning Åland Islands between Sweden and Finland or the arrangement of South Tyrol in 1946.

An autonomous regime may have the right to appeal or get supervision from an international organization. These measures were available to Åland for approaching the League of Nations and for Memel, the International Court of Justice.

Autonomy and Sovereignty

The issue of sovereignty is always part of the game between state and autonomous regions where the central government uses its power to prevent the regional authorities from gaining more power and the autonomous group struggles to get more authority over its areas. The central government fears that the regional power gain leads to secession and an independent sovereign state, whereas the autonomous regime asserts for more power over its resources and to preserve its national identity. The notion of sovereignty and absolute political power has been used by dictators and totalitarian regimes to justify complete authority over their people and the country. The rulers of medieval times used sovereignty to consolidate the power over their territories and maintained the external influence reaching to their regions.

The sovereignty of the state started to establish during the Holy Roman Empire, and the theory of sovereignty had a huge impact on the state hierarchy in early modern Europe. The emergence of federalism and democracy in the twentieth century significantly weakened the concept of sovereignty. The notion of absolute power and who was the sovereign of state hierarchy began to change from the vertical to the horizontal form of government, and people became the supreme authority of a state. The American Declaration of Independence on 1776 brought up the concept of popular sovereignty, meaning the people are the authority who invest their power in their representatives and government. The sovereignty is entrusted to the federal structure of the United States. In 1791, the French asserted that the nation is power and sovereign of the state. For John Austin, the sovereignty was invested in the nation's parliament, which exercised the power on behalf of them (Lapidoth 1997).

It is believed that a state has obligations and agreements under international law that may restrict the sovereignty of the state in case of breaching certain rules of international norms. These kinds of restrictions began in the twentieth century when the international community had taken some measures against the use of force by the state to curb the struggle of people within. In recent times, the sovereignty of state has also been compromised and its jurisdiction restricted, and international actors intervened in the state's domestic issues of human rights and the development of the right of self-determination. State sovereignty has been challenged in terms of governing, acting with other states, and treating its citizens in its discretion. These authorities of the state have been limited according to new economic and constitutional international legal laws. As pointed out by Lapidoth (1997), a state is no longer completely free to handle its matters as it wishes. In the case of the right to self-determination and struggle for that purpose, it cannot be suppressed by force or other undemocratic means by any sovereign states. In such situations, the state has to agree in some kind of power-sharing or otherwise ultimately go through disintegration.

Cultural Autonomy

Cultural autonomy constitutes the power of cultural affairs of the minority groups. This is a limited autonomy granted to a minority group to run their cultural affairs. It comprises the uniqueness of their culture and language, and they are also empowered to handle their educational matters without the interference of central government. The purpose of this kind of autonomy is to let the minority group establish language and culture freely by themselves. However, it is not necessary to grant more power to the autonomous region. Cultural autonomy is not a path to separation or segregation but a right to preserve their culture, language, and identity according to internationally recognized legal rules (Heintze 1998).

Estonian cultural autonomy during the interwar period can be seen as a good example of cultural autonomy. It is a common trend that state governments make false promises to their minority groups—such as they will protect their identity and cultures and meet all their needs—but this is not always the case, although the Estonian government offered its minority groups the same kind of rights and assured them by legalizing these rights. The cultural right of minorities was adopted through legislation in 1925, giving identity rights to any ethnic group who had at least three thousand members or more. The legislation opened the way for Germans, Swedes, and Russians to keep their separate identity. The distinctive group membership was self-defined by the group that elected an authority to run its public affairs. These authorities could operate in the field of culture, education, libraries, museums, theaters, and sports. Because of the 1925 legislation, the Estonian German minority developed their cultural council. A new example can be seen in the rights of Sami in Finland. The Finnish constitutional act of August 1, 1995, gave the right to Sami to establish their separate authority. The constitution regarded Sami as indigenous people who shall enjoy the right to promote and preserve their language and culture (Heintze 1998).

Federalism and Autonomy

Sometimes a federal government can help to solve the differences between various ethnic groups in the state. A population of different ethnic and linguistic groups may form a national spirit by their own will, but not by the force or will of the central government. Federalism is a recognition of these groups as part of the state-governing bodies by accepting their regional authorities in the local legislation, judiciary, and administration. It is all about the power-sharing arrangement and the cooperation among the state units. The main role of the central government is to keep the federation together by consulting all units of the governing bodies of the federation. A federal system means holding all parts of the country intact in a balanced and cooperative manner. A constituent is considered to be one of the decision-making organs of the federal system, and the division of power is complex and requires constant balancing scrutiny from all authorities of the federation. Because a federal framework is based on the voluntary association of all groups, in the case of intense disagreement, it may fall apart (Heintze 1998).

There is a difference between federal systems and the rule of arrangement in a federal state. A federation means that a state is constitutionally divided into many regions that are called with different names. For example, in the United States, they are called state; in Germany, land; in Canada, province; and so on. The constitution arranges the power-sharing methods between central and regional governments. The entities are agreed in establishing the federation where they participate with central authorities for legislation and their representatives are also the members of the upper house. Any amendment of the federal constitution has to win the approval of regional parliaments. There has to be some kind of special board for resolving disputes between regions and central authority. The federation should work as an apolitical organization that keeps different parts of the country united under a larger political system. An autonomous area also may fall under the federal arrangement, but there are differences between autonomy and a federal government. Autonomy can be recognized and developed by constitutional changes or by an agreement or by both of them, whereas a federation is principally established by a constitution. In most cases, autonomy is granted to some particular areas where ethnic groups have their historical base in those regions. But the federal system is applied throughout the country, and all regions would enjoy their authorities under the central government. For autonomy, there is no special board or tribunal to deal with differences between the central and autonomous regions. A federation is mostly based on a territorial power-sharing mechanism, whereas autonomy can be considered a personalizing type of system, although federalism and autonomy may be combined at times. For example, the former Soviet Union and Yugoslavia were a part of the federal system but later also adopted the autonomous entities. These autonomous regions were not considered to be fully federal components. There are significant differences between autonomy and federalism, but some common points spread through the power-sharing mechanism (Lapidoth 1997).

Federalism of an ethnic nature constitutes a political and territorial mechanism of power-sharing such as the former Soviet Union. The various groups had their territorial right to government and self-decision-making methods. When the union collapsed, fifteen new sovereign states emerged on the map of the former Soviet Union. The breakdown of the Soviet Union is a different debate and was not a failure of the federalism per se but rather the failure of communism. The principle of federalism is a certain privilege and recognition of these groups and their respective territories. The federal structure is useful for easing tension among different groups of people in a country (Heintze 1998).

The Belgian federal guideline of 1994 was designed to meet a high degree of territorial-based structure of the state on the linguistic lines. The UN Security Council also passed similar federal methods for Cyprus in the resolution 939 (1994), stating that "Its position that a Cyprus settlement must be based on a state of Cyprus with a single sovereignty and international personality and single citizenship, with its independence and territorial integrity, safeguarded, and comprising two politically equal communities as described in the relevant Security Council resolutions, in a bi-communal and bi-zonal federation, and that such a settlement must exclude union in whole or in part with any other country or any form of partition or secession."

A federal state may help to settle the differences of people to allow them to live together in peace with equal respect. The federal method was used in the Washington Agreement, forming the Federation of Bosnia and Herzegovina in 1994. This kind of state structure may serve the purposes of ending ethnic conflicts and bring the battling groups to one table. A large community can live peacefully in a federation if they share common interests, values, and equal treatment. The true will of the central government for power-sharing may bring peace and respect among different groups. However, it will not guarantee that these groups will integrate and stay together in a federal system, specifically when the central government exercises a one-nation formula. A multiethnic federal state is not considered to be homogenous, but different people and groups form a voluntary will of a nation. The federation plays the most important role in terms of managing to mediate the differences among various groups through a federal order. The extensive decentralization provides an opportunity for minority groups to participate in mainstream politics. The federation of many groups requires a great deal of will of unity and power structure to sustain its viability. Canada and Switzerland can be a good example of this kind of governing system. Lapidoth (1997) observed that the decentralization of power implies some restricted power to the other units under the central government. There are different degrees of decentralization that may vary in their range of local authorities and the limit of central supervision. The devolution of power means handing out a certain amount of power to some areas, whereas autonomy is considered to be a power transfer method to a region. In the case of decentralization, local authorities may exercise some limited power, whereas an autonomous region enjoys the most of its power through locally elected representatives. Decentralized powers may be repealed unilaterally by the central government, whereas a change in the principle of autonomy requires the consent of the autonomous region.

It seems there is not much difference between self-government and autonomy where a group or community runs its territorial affairs without external interference. The meaning of self-government has been argued under article 73 of the UN Declaration Regarding Non-Self-Governing Territories. The United Nations have a responsibility for those who have not yet attained self-governing powers to protect and promote their rights and make sure inhabitants are treated equally. The UN is "to ensure, with due respect for the culture of the peoples concerned, their political, economic, social, and educational advancement, their just treatment, and their protection against abuses." The UN Declaration was designed to promote self-government of people and urges states for decentralization of power and to respect the rights of local populations (Lapidoth 1997, 52). Despite being similar concepts, self-government and autonomy differ from each other in many dimensions. For example, self-government is mostly related to a degree of self-rule, whereas the concept of autonomy is more flexible, covering from some limited to wide-ranging powers.

Autonomy has also been in the central debate in the United Nations for decades. UN General Assembly agreed that the method of self-rule may be a good reason for the right to self-determination in various circumstances. It was suggested that the idea of self-government was not to undermine or limit the concept of self-determination but to recommend additional support and harmonize its realization. The idea reached the United Nations in 1994, as a draft convention was submitted in the United Nations bringing forward the notion of self-determination through self-rule. The provision of the convention was shaped to promote the right of those distinctive groups of people who possess a particular area within a country to run their matters by self-government. When it is recognized that such a group of people inhabits the country, the state would have to accept the rights of these people and grant them the right to practice their values, culture, and language. The members of the group should also have the right to participate in public affairs and take part in regional and central elections. The community should be allowed to protect its interests in the public arena. These people would have the right to participate in various government institutions, including administration, policymaking, and relevant state funds. The involvement and consent of the group would be necessary regarding the decision-making that may affect their interests directly. Although in later times the community may consider having its sovereign and separate state and take this issue further to gain self-determination.

In some situations, it has been a successful method of arrangement between different parties. There is great hope that it will provide a more positive result in the future in terms of conflict solutions. In our modern world, the old ways of governments would not work for the people, and they will not rest until their rights are realized. It seems the world has been responding to this issue in numerous ways of political changes in the system of states. Apart from other political approaches, the concept of autonomy and its emergence through a democratic system of state has been a great change in the structure of the state power. The method of power-sharing may not be able to settle all political issues of the world, but without a doubt, it has been congruent to many cases and will be accommodating to a wide range of political arrangements in the future. The different forms of autonomy or decentralization of power can be used in the cases of minorities, indigenous, and ethnic disputes around the globe. The internationalization of these kinds of power-sharing methods and the support of the international community have been a huge change in the behavior of totalitarian states.

CHAPTER SIX

SOURCES OF INTERNATIONAL LAW

The sources of law have been generated throughout human history comprising tradition, treaty, custom, and general principles of legal rules. When states developed as entities, they adopted some of these norms as the rule of law to regulate their public and foreign affairs with other states. The question about the sources of law is always a fundamental issue for the legal concept whether it is domestic or international. Sources of law define the legal foundation of a society and nation. In the contemporary world, the question of international law is the greatest concern of the international community that seems to be focused on justifying its legal matters according to a modern community of nations.

The theory of natural and positive law has evolved during the fifteenth and sixteenth centuries, navigating their way into the international legal order through the League of Nations and the United Nations after the Second World War. Since the Great Wars, the sources of international law have witnessed far-reaching changes. With the formation of the United Nations, international law has expanded its area of jurisdiction by including individual rights in the international legal order, which brought new measures for the sovereign states. The adoption of individual rights in international legal methods has challenged the sovereignty of states and given protection to human rights. The contemporary international laws are generated through conventions, treaties, and decisions of the International Court of Justice and adopted by the international community as rules of the world.

Natural Law

The natural phenomena are ruled by nature and applied according to human logic and understanding. Natural law is based on moral principles of human conduct, and these laws are preexistent to the modern rule of law. The natural principles of law are the basis of our modern institutionalized national or international law. Famous international lawyer Emer de Vattel (1714–1767) theorized that if states contribute in an equal manner in their relations, they can benefit from it and may secure one another's interests. For Vattel, the natural law not only was a source of bringing states to respect the existence of one another but also to assist in various conditions. He explained that it was simply the natural law of people applied to states. There are some legal rules that states agree with one another to follow to maintain their relations; Vattel called them the necessary law of nations. He defined three kinds of positive laws, calling them the voluntary law, which is supposed to be in the form of some kind of agreement; the conventional law, which carries an expression of consent, and the customary law, which is the tacit consent. This kind of concept and trichotomy of law was expressed in article 38 (1) of the Statute of the International Court of Justice concerning its general principles of law from conventions to the customary legal norms. The concept of law reflects on what the law is and how it should be and how it should operate in the world arena. As stressed by Degan (1997), it is very important to identify the theory and the practice of law in both dimensions, domestic and international level. It would help us to understand the nature of law and its validity in the modern world.

Dutch legal scholar Hugo Grotius introduced a political and moral standard of international law, relating it to state sovereignty and international relations. He believed that as a community benefits from the rule of law, nations can be harmonized under certain international principles. According to him, there are few forms of laws; the law applies to a small entity, and the law applies to a larger entity. The small entity meaning a province or region of a country, and larger can apply to a state or the entire world. Generally, the law concerns what a person, nation, country, or international community owe to each other. He examined law and ethics, explaining how they differ and intertwine with each other (Grotius 2018). His law was generated by courts, states, government and treaties, and other organizations, but his ethical rules seemed to come from some form of affection, loyalty, tradition human reasoning, and logic of rightness. He regarded the theory of natural law as the essence of human understanding and reasoning and that it's written in the heart of every human being. John Locke (1632–1704) also observed the natural right of a free man in his *Two Treatises of Government*. He defined the legal rights to life and liberty in a just society where men are free and equal and entrust some of their rights to the government to establish a comfortable society where they all enjoy their lives and liberty. He advocated that if a government fails to protect the right and liberty of its citizens, then that government should be replaced by its people. His theory was based on natural law and the natural rights of people.

Positive Law

Positive law is based on human-made laws through state legislation, courts, or other national and international institutions. The statutory rules of law are established by some authorities, laying down some specific rights and responsibilities for people and states to follow. The Peace Treaty of Westphalia in 1648 greatly influenced the establishment of state practice in Europe. The treaty paved the way for international methods between states during the nineteenth century and is considered to be one of the founding agreements concerning state security and sovereignty. The doctrine of positive rules of law was thought to be the will of a state, but on the other hand, a state could not exist on its own and without the help of other states. Thereby, the will of a state manifested itself into the will of all states and nations. The will of all states had to accept a universal system that would allow them to exercise their affairs within the international law, which resulted in all states coming under a superior world order. However, the doctrine of voluntarisms proved to be insufficient during World War II. The judges of Nürenberg trials during 1945–1946 could not grant their verdicts on the principles of the law of consent from any country, including Germany and Japan. The court had to develop the responsibility of those involved in a crime against humanity who denied a whole group of people the right to existence. The court stated that an act of genocide is not an evil act because of a positive rule of international law; it is a heinous crime itself against humanity, and civilized nations have a responsibility to punish those who commit such evil crimes. It seems relying only on a set of positive international rules would reduce the wide nature of international principles. The International Court of Justice has also used the basis of equitability for its decisions rather than a strict application of the law in many cases. Therefore, international lawyers believe that the general principle of international rules is important for a comprehensive justice system (Degan 1997). Article 38 (1) of the International Court of Justice (ICJ) has recognized various principles of law and their legality, authority, and sources, including conventions, treaties, and general principles of the law of nations. The role of the court has increased since codification began in 1945. During 1950, the International Law Commission (ILC) recommended a list of sources of international law, including treaties, customary rules, rulings of the International Court of Justice, and decisions of international organizations (Besson and d'Aspremont 2017).

Customary Law

Customary law is evolved through human behavior and customs. There is a sequence of actions that have been always adopted and accepted as law by communities throughout the history of mankind. The wide range of customary rules has also been established as a universal pattern and recognized as international legal norms in various conditions. The general concept of customary law is believed to be a separate form and source of law, but it is not completely true as it can take a form of treaty law and also remain a separate mechanism to fill gaps of international law in different situations. The customary principles of international law have evolved throughout history. The powerful inducement of customary rules came through treaties and conventions. Article 1 (2) of the UN Charter common to both covenants has bestowed bringing general rules into the treaties and promoting states to adopt and respect those general rules of law equally. All member states of the UN and the international community came to understand the importance of the covenants for peace and security in our world and committed themselves to the universal rule, such as the right to self-determination of people. The course of their action and behavior gradually had formed a general system of legal principles, bringing all countries on board and respecting the international common norms. It was necessary to bring powerful and weak states into an internationally recognized system of obligations; thereby, the international legal methods were laid down in the UN General Assembly (Cassese 1995).

Treaty Law

The law of treaty is mainly based on the agreements between states and international organizations. These kinds of legally binding contracts are known as a pact, covenant, or protocol and are conventions that are agreed by various actors and play a significant role internationally. These kinds of international conventions began to unfold during World War I and resulted in the Vienna Convention on the Law of Treaties in 1969. Powerful states such as the United Kingdom, the Soviet Union, and the United States have begun negotiation for an international organization far earlier in 1943.

The United Kingdom, USA, USSR, and Chinese representatives started a secret dialogue in 1944 at Dumbarton Oaks to establish an international organization. They came up with various suggestions for a United Nations from the Dumbarton Oaks Conference. The Dumbarton Oaks Conference established the paragraph 4 of the Moscow Declaration of 1943. The conference delegations from the Soviet Union, China, the United States, and the United Kingdom deliberated on the idea of establishing an organization for peace and security. The Third Moscow Conference was the first step forward where foreign ministers of big powers—including the United States, the Soviet Union, and the United Kingdom—met and discussed the matters of the world. These key players recognized the need for collaboration for a peaceful purpose and to put an end to warring nations. The Moscow Declaration was put forward by Premier Joseph Stalin of the Soviet Union, Prime Minister Winston Churchill, and United States president Franklin Roosevelt. They also agreed to set up a European Advisory Commission that suggested democracy for Italy, Greece, and independent Austria (Pubantz and Moore Jr. 2008).

In 1945, the four great powers agreed to develop friendly relations among nations at the San Francisco Conference on the basis of respecting the principle of equal rights and self-determination of peoples. Most members of the conference agreed that the rule of self-determination is one of the safest paths to peace and security in the new emerging world. Despite some of the opposing members, the principle of self-determination was adopted as a treaty for the first time in the conference, and it was suggested that all states must respect the right of self-determination. To regulate international treaties, the Vienna Convention on the Law of Treaties was established in 1969. Since then, there have been numerous international agreements and conventions relating to human rights and the sovereignty of states (Cassese 1995).

The Role of the International Court of Justice

The International Court of Justice (ICJ), or the World Court, is the judicial organ of the United Nations. The court is one of the most important arms of the Security Council, playing a crucial role in maintaining the world's peace and security. The main role of the court is to settle international disputes among states and give advisory opinions and judgments on legal matters of the world. The decisions of the United Nations General Assembly and the judgments of the International Court of Justice are the backbones of international law (Thirlway 2016).

The preparation for an international court had begun during the Hague Conventions of 1899 and 1907, which was followed by the establishment of the Permanent Court of International Justice (PCIJ) in 1922 under the League of Nations. After the failure of the League of Nations to avert the Second World War, the international community was obligated to take immediate action in this regard. The League of Nations was replaced by the United Nations on

October 24, 1945, and the old court by the International Court of Justice in February 1946 (Kolb 2013). The powers of the International Court of Justice are somewhat similar to the old Permanent Court of International Justice, as the charter is based on the statute of the old court. However, in its new chapter, the court has provided some great changes in the international legal system and established a strong place in the heart of the international community.

Article 21 of the Rome Statute of the International Criminal Court plainly defines a hierarchy of relevancy of the law, and article 38 supports the international legal norm in its range and application. The clause tends to give the court a system to practice and watch over the mutual obligations of states in terms of their international attitude toward international law. The reference to article 38 of the statute of the court bears international custom as evidence of a general practice accepted as law. The general practice of the International Court of Justice recognizes that the international legal order is the responsibility of all states in their practice (Brownlie 2008).

The international legal system was fragile during the Cold War, but since the collapse of the Soviet Union, there has been some progress in the international legal order. With the dissolution of the Soviet Union, states and governments realized that the United Nations was gaining a firm foothold in the international affairs of the world; they began to shift their allegiance toward the United Nations. The pattern of international rules was mutually recognized by the international community and became legal principles of the modern world. According to these rules, all states are equal members of the international union and are equally responsible for their behavior toward these norms. Failure to meet the international legal standards may result in exclusion from the respected community of the world. Chapter 7 of the United Nations authorizes the Security Council to determine any form of action against those states that are involved in any kind of breach of the international legal order. The International Court of Justice has been playing a great role alongside other organs of the United Nations for the last fifty years. The court made significant progress in internationalizing the universal principles of law. The court has been greatly serving the international interests of states and mankind in its various capacities, but the international legal system is far from being perfect.

All sources of law are fundamental to any human society, as they play an essential role in legal reasoning and decision-making. The sources of international laws are based on the same pattern of human behavior, but they are designed to harmonize a larger community under some universal principles of law. These sources of law tend to generate a wide range of legal methods for international law and provide support for filling the gap of law in certain areas. The inherited theory of law from last generations provides the base and right direction for an international legal system, but they are unable to meet the new challenges of the constantly changing world in their old forms. It is crucial to understand the law and its allocation in any society or on a universal level. The most important rule of international law is about human rights, and these rights have been promoted and protected in numerous conventions of the United Nations. The international rule of law is crucial for human rights protection and prevention of violence. When the rights of individuals were adopted in international law, all states became accountable for their human rights violations.

THE PRINCIPLE OF THE RIGHT OF SELF-DETERMINATION AND THE UN

The Case of East Timor, Eritrea, South Sudan, Western Sahara, and Bangladesh

During the decolonization of the world from European powers in the 1950s, some regions and national entities were either amalgamated into new countries against the will of the people or left on the mercy of their neighboring countries. For them, on the departure of Western powers, the colonial rules were replaced by stronger states in these regions. These nations were invaded again and faced even worse colonial measures than the former Western occupiers. However, in some cases, the international community came to their rescue, and they got their freedom with the help of the United Nations—except for Bangladesh, which was able to obtain the ultimate support of India in the form of humanitarian intervention in 1971. The case of Western Sahara is still pending despite the resolution of the United Nations, the ruling of the International Court of Justice, and the official support of the African Union for a referendum. This chapter sheds some light on the independent movements of East Timor, Eritrea, South Sudan, Western Sahara, and Bangladesh through a brief case study of their journey to the right of self-determination.

The Chinese arrived in East Timor in the thirteenth century looking for sandalwood, but the region was free from colonization until the fifteenth century. During 1497–1499, the first Portuguese voyage of Vasco da Gama to India opened its doors of influence throughout Southeast Asia. The famous Portuguese voyage through sea connected Europe to Asia was meant to be focused on trades but resulted in colonizing a vast area of the world from Asia to Africa and beyond. East Timor came under the Portuguese rule in 1586. On the departure of the Portuguese on November 28, 1975, East Timor was invaded by Indonesia, and it gained independence on August 30, 1999, through a referendum.

The Eritrean region became part of the Ethiopian Empire during the eleventh and nineteenth centuries. Italian forces invaded the region of Eritrea in 1881, and Ethiopia accepted the Italian occupation over the region by signing the Treaty of Wichale in 1889. Eritrea remained under Italian control until Italy was defeated by Allies forces in 1941. Thereafter, the area came under the control of the United Kingdom; and on the departure of Great Britain, despite the resistance of Eritrean people, the region was amalgamated with Ethiopia in 1952. However, after a long political and armed struggle—with the involvement of the United Nations—the Eritrean people were given the right to choose their political status and became an independent state through a referendum under the supervision of the United Nations in April 1993.

South Sudan came under the Ottoman Empire in 1820. The purpose of the Ottoman advances in the region was to bring more wealth and slaves to Cairo. The Egyptian administrations moved the office of the regional governor general to Khartoum in 1835. Later, Sudan came under the Anglo-Egyptian control from 1899 to 1956; the period of rule is known as Anglo-Egyptian Condominium, the joint government of the region. However, in reality, it was the British who ruled the region. The geographical location of Sudan lying between the Middle East and Africa gave birth to various issues. The differences of language, culture, and religion were used to break their unity and rule over them. United Sudan had fought against colonial powers and achieved its independence in 1956, but the dream of a united Sudan faded away during decades of civil wars and bloodshed. South Sudan broke away from Khartoum in 2011 and became another independent country in the Horn of Africa.

It seems that the process of decolonization of Western Sahara is extending toward an uncharted direction since the Europeans departed from Africa. Western Sahara is situated on the northwest African coastline, which is surrounded by Morocco to the north, Algeria to the northeast, and Mauritania to the east and south. During the European colonization in 1884, the area came under the Spanish rule. When Morocco gained freedom from France in 1956, it began to claim its rule over Western Sahara. On the other hand, Algeria and Mauritania also claimed their sovereignty over the Sahrawi region. The United Nations called for a referendum in 1975, and the International Court of Justice also gave its ruling in the favor of the Sahrawi people, but they are still waiting for the right to be realized.

The early history of Bengal can be traced back to seventh century BC. Through its long history, the old Bengal had seen numerous kingdom and dynasties. The region became part of the Mughal Empire in 1526. When the Mughal Empire began to tumble during 1700, Bengal became an autonomous region and remained united under the leadership of Nawab Siraj-ud-Daulah until he was defeated by the British East India Company in 1757. The East India Company gradually turned into the British Raj and colonized the entire Indian subcontinent for two hundred years. When the British Empire began to decline after the Second World War, it divided India in the name of religion in 1947. East Bengal was amalgamated into the new state of Pakistan and became part of the religious state. However, after two decades of suffering a bloody conflict ensued with dominant West Pakistan. With the help of India, East Pakistan emerged on the map of the world as an independent state of Bangladesh in 1971.

East Timor

Brief History of East Timor

The history of East Timor is full of occupations, abandonment, and neglect. A small half of an island, about four hundred miles on the northwest of Australia, with a population of one million people, the territory is a mountainous region, rainy in winter and dry in summer. East Timor was not one of those resourceful regions where powerful nations could be focused and interested, but despite its destitution, it had gone through conflict and destruction for decades. The small island was invaded by various conquerors, but it became one of the Portuguese colonies during 1586. Many nations around the globe have gone through a similar struggle for centuries to achieve their freedom, but some nations have suffered more than their share for realizing their dreams. The island has been divided into two parts, East and West Timor. The eastern part had been a Portuguese colony since 1586. The western part of the island had been under Dutch control and became part of Indonesia after its independence in 1946. East Timor was declared independent on November 28, 1975, after the departure of Portuguese, but shortly after that, it was invaded and occupied by Indonesia on December 7, 1975. Since then, it was under the brutal rule of Indonesia until its independence in 2002 (Ronen 2011).

Portuguese Rule

During the reign of King João III of Portugal, the search for new routes and trades expanded to Southeast Asia, reaching East Timor. The first Portuguese settlement began to develop in East Timor in 1633, which was the beginning of European and Christian faith in that part of the world. The Portuguese faced the Indonesian rebellion in the sixteenth century and later the opposition of the Netherlands. When the Dutch gained independence from Spain in 1581, they sustained their influence throughout Indonesia during the early seventeenth century (Ballard 2008).

The Portuguese maintained their position over the eastern part of the island but did not rule directly until 1701. They assigned Antonio Coelho Guerreiro, a rich merchant, as the governor of the region. He was granted all powers by the viceroy of Goa to impose law and order by whatever means he believed appropriate. Coelho Guerreiro endeavored to establish a civil and judicial system with a regular military that could have the strength to hold on to its possessions in the area. The great distance of the empire from the capital and the Portuguese possession of Goa made it difficult for the governor to communicate and seek assistance on time and need. He was isolated from the entire Portuguese empire and had to deal with regional opposing groups and tribal leaders (Ballard 2008). However, the rebellion erupted against Portuguese rule during the eighteenth century. As revolt intensified, the capital was moved from Lifao to Dili in 1769, and rebel forces took control of Lifao and surrounding areas. On the other hand, the Dutch and Portuguese rivalry went on in Indonesia. The Dutch kept the pressure on the Portuguese but was not that much interested in the small part of islands controlled by them. The dispute regarding the borders continued for decades without any solution. In 1893, they reached to some kind of division in Timor; and by 1904, they signed an agreement in Hague confirming the controlled areas (Ballard 2008).

The situation in Timor began to be aggravated during 1907. The Timorese people never adopted the occupation of Portuguese in terms of confirming the rules of colonial administration. East Timor was governed by two systems: one was the local governing body and the other was the Portuguese administration in the region. The head tax of Portuguese administration in 1908 was considered to be yet another attempt to undermine the power of local chiefs. This kind of action from the colonial government increased tension between indigenous Timorese and the Portuguese administration (Ballard 2008). The uprising began with the insult of a local tribal chief by the Portuguese administration, and the administrator was killed because of that incident by local people. The unrest took the Portuguese administration one and a half years to suppress. The Portuguese changed their ruling patterns from ruling with an iron fist to more lenient methods and established a civil governing body in Dili (Ballard 2008).

World War II in Timor

During the Second World War, a wave of army movements in 1942 brought more misery to East Timor. The Netherlands and Australian armed forces landed in the region to prevent the Japanese from advancing further. Despite that, Japanese troops invaded the small Portuguese colony in February and continued their battle to conquer more land, expanding their strategic positions in Southeast Asia. The Battle of Singapore was won by the Japanese, and they took over the stronghold of the British and had supremacy in the region. On the other hand, the Dutch also gave up their possessions to the

Japanese without any resistance. For the Australian, the small island was strategically important for their own country, so they continued to resist the aggressor in small groups with local assistance until the end (Ballard 2008).

The end of the Second World War in 1945 brought back the Portuguese and the Timorese struggle for freedom. The new phase of East Timor also brought up the Indonesian interests on the island as they pushed for their independent state. The Indonesians considered the territory belonged to them and should be included in the future state of Indonesia. During 1950–1960s, the Portuguese changed their way of governing the province. These methods were appointing local administrative bodies to run their local affairs under the Portuguese empire. Education through the Catholic Church became the key to bring most of the Timorese closer to Portuguese influence. Thereby, for the first time, Lisbon attempted to improve the life of local Timorese with some financial help and through employing a legislative council for the region in 1963. During these five years, there were some development in East Timor that had never happened before (Ballard 2008).

When the Second World War ended, it brought forward a wave of demand for independence and decolonization in Portuguese-held regions in various parts of the world. The uprising began in Portuguese Africa from Angola, Guinea-Bissau, to Mozambique. The Portuguese sent thousands of troops to Africa to control the situation but failed, and these kinds of uprisings gained momentum throughout the world. As the Portuguese empire started to tumble, the Timorese struggle for freedom also increased its efforts to be recognized. However, the upheaval in other colonies of the empire was more powerful than the small island of Timor; and for a while, Timor was not on the screens of relevant powers.

Tumbling Portuguese Empire

The military coup of April 25, 1974, changed the Portuguese power game within and throughout its colonies. The coup in Lisbon soon followed by the popular movement of civil resistance that led to toppling the regime of Estado Novo and the withdrawal of Portuguese forces from Africa and East Timor. As the Portuguese empire began to collapse, the resistance movements gained momentum in all colonies from Africa to East Timor. There were three parties in East Timor. The Timorese Democratic Union (UDT) was a pro-Portuguese organization but later changed its position from the association to an independent Timor for Timorese people. The Timorese Social Democratic Association (ASDT) supported rather a gradual decolonization, lasting a decade. During these years, they expected political, economic, and social development in the region. The third and smallest group was the Timorese Popular Democratic Association, or APOD, (advocating for the integration of Timor into Indonesia), which was believed to be an Indonesian-sponsored group (Ballard 2008).

The Portuguese administration in East Timor developed some methods for gradual decolonization but faced new emerging opposition from the party that had supported the idea until then. The declining power of the Portuguese administration opened the doors for new political dimensions. Thereby, the Timorese Social Democratic Association changed its gradual decolonization approach into an immediate independence demand. The organization was renamed Revolutionary Front for an Independent East Timor (FRETILIN). The situation in East Timor became difficult to manage for the Portuguese who were striving to sustain their possession of the region. On the other hand, UDT didn't only change its pro-Portuguese tactic to freedom of East Timor but began its attacks against FRETILIN forces. UDT captured Dili on December 7, 1975, and imprisoned FRETILIN fighters. These two groups striving for independence of East Timor kept fighting against each other in different parts of the island.

As the difference between local forces widened and the region was slipping toward a civil war, the Portuguese called on all parties for negotiations. When Portuguese authorities failed to bring these warring factions around the table, they moved their base to Atauro Island. The Portuguese administration in East Timor was losing its grip over the region. The FRETILIN forces declared the independence of East Timor, but UDT, APODETI, and Portuguese rejected the FRETILIN's unilateral declaration of independence. Indonesian forces were watching these chaotic events very closely in East Timor and marched into East Timor on December 7, 1975. The Indonesian government claimed that the situation in East Timor was destabilizing the whole region. The real reason to invade East Timor was not only this but they also always believed that East Timor was an integral part of their country. Furthermore, many analysts believe the Indonesian invasion was the result of some kind of understanding between the United States and Indonesia, as it happened right after the meeting of presidents Gerald Ford and Suharto on December 6, 1975, in Jakarta. It is understood that the US support to the Suharto regime in that high times of Cold War may have been a counterstrategy against communist influence in East Timor because the revolutionary forces of FRETILIN were communist-influenced and the US was supplying weapons to Indonesian armed forces (Ballard 2008).

East Timor Case in United Nations

After the Indonesian invasion on East Timor, the Portuguese administration withdrew from its post immediately. Indonesia confirmed the territory as its twenty-seventh province on July 17, 1976, despite the United Nations' declared support to the right of self-determination of East Timorese people. Portugal took the matter to the United Nations on December 22, 1975. The UN Security Council voted against the Indonesian actions in East Timor. The United Nations stated that the East Timorese people have a right to self-determination and independence according to the UN Charter and their inalienable rights must be respected. Thereby, the UN demanded the immediate withdrawal of Indonesian forces from the region. After four months of the Indonesian invasion of East Timor, the UN Security Council passed resolution 389, endorsing the right of self-determination of East Timorese people and calling for Indonesian occupying forces to leave East Timor. The UN General Assembly passed resolutions from 1976 to 1982 calling for the right of self-determination of East Timorese people, but the United States and China did not agree stronger action against Indonesia (Ballard 2008).

In 1982, the UN secretary-general called on all parties involved in the case of East Timor to find a tangible solution for the worsening situation in the region. Many legal experts agreed that Indonesia was in breach of international law by invading East Timor and denying the right of self-determination of East Timorese people. They argued that the United Nations must protect the international legal order and provide the right of self-determination to Timorese people. Despite the international opposition, Indonesia continued to establish its grip on the territory, ignoring all UN resolutions.

Indonesian Invasion and Genocide

Indonesia has always claimed that East Timor is its territory until it seized the chance to invade the region on December 7, 1975. Suharto was watching carefully the decreasing Portuguese influence over its colonies. It was obvious that the empire was falling apart and the decolonization was on its way to all Portuguese colonies. While Portugal was facing difficulties to maintain its control over colonies, Suharto decided to meet US president Ford and Kissinger in Camp David on July 5, 1975, to show his friendship with the US and discuss the situation of the region. On the one hand, Suharto showed that he was a friend of the USA; and on the other hand, he seemed to convince them that East Timor would not be a viable state. Thereby, it is believed that he got the green signal from the US president to do what was best for his country and the region. Besides, the US administration considered FRETILIN as a communist group. After six months of that meeting, Indonesian armed forces invaded East Timor (Kiernan 2008).

Portugal protested against the Indonesian invasion and took the matter to the United Nations. The United Nations had already recognized the island as a non-self-governing region in 1960, and Portugal had been promoting the right of self-determination of Timorese since it departed from the area. Portugal took a stand that the Indonesian invasion blocked the chance of Timorese people to freely choose their political future. The truth of the matter was that East Timorese were not allowed to express their free and genuine will under free and fair supervision of the United Nations. The decision of integration with Indonesia was made by an appointed and pro-Indonesian provincial assembly under the shadow of the occupying military forces of Indonesia. The decision of merger with Indonesia was not made directly by the people of East Timor; thereby, it was baseless. The denial of self-determination to East Timor was a breach of international law and general rules of the UN and its resolution 1514 (XV), which grants the colonial people to choose their destiny (Cassese 1995).

From the day of invasion to the last day of its occupation, the Indonesian forces practiced the most brutal methods to control the area. They randomly slaughtered the East Timor population because of their ethnicity and political demand for self-determination. According to various reports, the Indonesian military committed genocide in East Timor. Besides the direct execution of East Timorese, Indonesian forces also used the deprivation of food, water, and medicine as a killing weapon. But the heinous crimes against humanity were only noticed by the international community when five Australian journalists were killed by Indonesian forces on October 16, 1975, in East Timor (Kiernan 2008, 109). The invading forces took drastic measures to cleanse the area of the separatist movements. Ballard mentioned a note from a British official:

The Indonesian themselves acknowledged that about 80,000 East Timorese died in the late 1970s, out of a population of 650,000. Some non-governmental organizations (NGOs) suggest as many as 200,000, or about one-third of the territory's population perished. Immediately after the invasion, East Timor's misery was compounded by a famine exacerbated by the policy of establishing strategic hamlets, and the consequent disruption of normal farming. Comparison of the last Portuguese and first Indonesian census, taking into account up to 40,000 East Timorese who fled abroad, suggests a minimum figure of over 100,000 deaths. (Ballard 2008, 10)

It is understood that 16 percent of East Timor's population perished during the Indonesian occupation. The heavy bombardment of Indonesian forces pushed the population back. However, the FRETILIN military wing continued its fighting against occupying forces of Indonesia. For the FRETILIN military wing, the mighty Indonesian army with sophisticated weapons was no match, and they couldn't engage them with a full-fledged war. They changed their way of resistance to guerrilla warfare. This was considered to be a wise decision from the FRETILIN leadership to sustain the resistance and campaign for international support and recognition. The guerrilla forces of FRETILIN focused on the Indonesian army movements in the area and launched targeted attacks in various zones. The FRETILIN revolt against Indonesian forces led by Nicolau Lobato between 1975 and 1978 managed to keep the occupying army in the big towns, and most of the rural areas were free from the Indonesian forces. But later in 1977, the Suharto administration intensified its attacks on guerrilla positions, destroying their camps and hideouts (Ballard 2008).

The heavy artillery of the Indonesian army almost finished the Armed Forces for the National Liberation of East Timor (FALINTIL) led by Xanana Gusmão. Their guerrilla wing was reduced from twenty-seven thousand to five thousand. The Indonesian armed forces did not only try to completely clean the territory from the guerrilla fighters but they also committed massacres during their indiscriminate shelling on East Timorese town and villages. However, despite being weak and exhausted, the resistance continued with its limited activities, keeping the Indonesians believe that the East Timorese will never accept their occupation. The situation of East Timor was exacerbated in 1977, as the Suharto regime pushed for more area, encompassing FALINTIL camps and clearing them of freedom fighters (Ballard 2008).

On December 31, 1978, the Indonesian army killed the prominent leader of Timorese people, Nicolau Lobato, along with many other key leaders, in an ambush on Mount Matebian. The Indonesian forces managed to destroy the main base of FRETILIN fighters in the mountains. Their huge number and heavy weaponry pushed the Timorese freedom fighters underground. When the Timorese leaders realized that they could not afford a confrontation with the Indonesian army, they changed their approach to handling the occupying forces. The death of Lobato and heavy casualties of guerilla fighters brought a difficult time for Timorese people. After that, the resistance was led by Xanana Gusmão. He became the leader of FALINTIL in 1981 (Ballard 2008).

Xanana Gusmão recognized the weakening position of the resistance and thereby agreed to a ceasefire in 1983. East Timorese began to reorganize their organizations and rebuild their relationship with the population, which was severely damaged by Indonesian massacres and displacement of the population. On the other hand, East Timorese resistance sought more support from the international community. United Nations had already recognized their right to self-determination and pushed Indonesia for talk and negotiations to find a peaceful solution for the conflict. As pressure built up on the Indonesian administration, they changed their tactics in East Timor. After a distracting campaign against the local population, they tried to win the heart of the East Timorese by starting some development schemes, but it was too late and too little to heal the wounds of the East Timorese (Ballard 2008).

The Catholic Church and Christian faith had been one of the strongest sources of hope for East Timorese people throughout their struggle for freedom, and to some extent, the Catholic Church became the identity of East Timorese people. The Suharto administration understood this and wanted to assure the Christian world that the small Christian population of East Timor would be protected under the Indonesian rule. Thereby, they agreed to welcome Pope John Paul II on October 12, 1989. The Indonesian were thinking that the pope's visit would be some kind of recognition of Indonesian rule over East Timor, but it seemed that Pope John Paul II's visit sparked hope for East Timorese as a nation and they gained even more international support for an independent East Timor (Ballard 2008).

East Timorese resistance under the leadership of Xanana Gusmão realized that without a united organization of all groups, they would not be able to send a strong message either to the Indonesian or the international community. In the 1990s, they came up with the idea of the National Council of Maubere Resistance (CNRM). This was an attempt to bring all groups under one umbrella against the Indonesian occupation. On the other hand, José Ramos-Horta never stopped knocking on the door of the United Nations. He was the voice of East Timorese people in exile, reminding the world that East Timorese are also human and entitled to have rights and choose their future. Because of his peaceful struggle for his people for decades, he was later rewarded the Nobel Peace Prize in 1996 (Ballard 2008).

The Indonesian Army was determined to keep people under control and could not even accept a peaceful demonstration. The massacre of Santa Cruz in 1991 by the Indonesian Armed Forces was a turning point for the world. The Indonesian Army opened fire on a peaceful demonstration, killing two hundred and injuring around 230. The outrage of the international community grew over the massacre of innocent civilians. The brutal action of the Suharto regime was condemned by the international community. Xanana Gusmão called for the world leaders to support Timorese people for their right to self-determination. It is believed that the massacre was the beginning of the end of Indonesian rule over East Timor (Ballard 2008, 13).

As pressure developed from Lisbon to the United Nations and in East Timor, Xanana Gusmão's campaign against Indonesian occupation and brutality developed. He was gaining wider public and international support. To sabotage his campaign, the Indonesian captured Xanana Gusmão in Dili in 1992, and he was sentenced to life imprisonment in 1993. His arrest aimed to curb the activity of FALINTIL in East Timor, and to some extent, the Indonesians weakened the resistance movement within, but it gained even more support worldwide. When the Nobel Peace Prize was awarded to two East Timorese prominent leaders José Ramos-Horta and Bishop Ximenes Belo in 1996, recognizing their work for justice and peace, the two winners of the Nobel Peace Prize from a small struggling nation of East Timor brought forward immediate attention to East Timor. The United Nations and many world leaders who were concerned and working for a peaceful solution for the conflict pushed for more support from the international community (Ballard 2008).

The Intervention of the United Nations

In December 1975, the UN General Assembly resolution 3485 (XXX) strongly condemned Indonesia on East Timor and called for an immediate withdrawal from the island and to let the inhabitants decide their destiny with free will. Indonesia was found in breach of international law by violating the self-determination of the Timorese people. Besides, the UN called on all states to respect the territorial integrity of East Timor as well as the right of self-determination of its inhabitants. The Indonesian act of invasion and occupation was regarded as illegal and against international law that was endorsed by the International Court of Justice in its judgment. It was also suggested that Indonesia was found in breach of article 1 of the UN Charter, which forbids all kinds of aggression and is not limited in its applicability to states (Ronen 2011).

The United Nations General Assembly passed various resolutions from 1975 to 1982 recognizing the inalienable right to self-determination of East Timorese people and condemning the illegal occupation of Indonesia over the region. The newly appointed UN secretary-general Kofi Annan selected a special rapporteur in 1997 for East Timor to bring forward a peaceful and acceptable plan for all parties involved in the conflict. Besides, Portugal and various other countries that were supporting the case of East Timor kept pushing for more and immediate action from the UN nations (Gunn 2010).

The situation of East Timor began to change when the long-ruling president of Indonesia, Suharto, resigned in 1998. Indonesia had been facing a hard time as the crippling economic sanctions and the pressure from the United Nations was mounting against Jakarta. On the other hand, US president Bill Clinton called on Suharto's successor, Bacharuddin Jusuf Habibie, to accept the international force in East Timor or brace his country for more problems. The new president of Indonesia had no choice but to agree with the United Nations' plans for East Timor. The UN Security Council approved an International Force East Timor (INTERFET), led by Australia, to restore security and provide humanitarian help. The UN-mandated international force arrived in East Timor in September 1999. After decades of suffering and uncertain future, the East Timorese were relieved to find the United Nations peacekeeping mission landing on their soil (Gunn 2010).

Indonesia, with its proxies, kept trying to hinder the work of international force in East Timor but faced intense pressure from the United Nations and European Union. After two decades and a half of ruling over East Timor, Indonesia agreed to a United Nations–backed referendum in East Timor. The United Nations Mission in East Timor (UNAMET) was structured to provide security and to supervise the referendum in East Timor. The referendum was held on August 30, 1999, and people overwhelmingly voted for an independent East Timor. At last, Xanana Gusmão was released from prison, and he became the first president of the Democratic Republic of East Timor in 2002. The first new nation of the century paid a huge price in their national struggle for freedom. After a long and traumatic journey, East Timor achieved its independence on May 20, 2002. The United Nations put a mission forward to build East Timor and help Timorese to overcome their painful history of the struggle for freedom (Gunn 2010, 20).

Eritrea

The Eritrean conflict and the question of the right to self-determination is one of the many around the world left unsolved by colonial powers until later times. The historical nature of the Eritrean conflict makes it a unique case in the Horn of Africa. Eritrea was colonized by Italy during the Scramble for Africa by European powers in 1881 and 1914. When Italy was defeated by Anglo-American forces in 1941, it gave up its ambition of colonizing Africa, signing out a Peace Treaty with Allies later in 1947. Thereby, Great Britain took control of Eritrea. Ethiopia claimed its sovereignty over the Eritrean territory. The claim of Ethiopians over Eritrea was based on its historical relationship with the Ethiopian Empire. However, Eritrea maintained its independence after a long political and armed struggle with the involvement of great powers, ultimately backing the right of self-determination of Eritrean people under the umbrella of the United Nations.

Historical Background

The history of Eritrea can be traced back to the Kingdom of Aksum in the first century BC, and then the region became part of the Ethiopian Empire during the eleventh and nineteenth centuries. The coastal area was controlled by Muslim rulers and the highland by Christians. In 1885, Italian marched into the region and occupied the territory of Eritrea. Through the Treaty of Wichale of 1889, Ethiopia accepted the Italian occupation over Eritrea. The Eritrean territory remained under Italian control and later became part of Italian Eastern Africa in 1936 when the Italian invaded Ethiopia. The Italian army entered Addis Ababa on May 5, 1936. Emperor Haile Selassie went into exile and called on the League of Nations for help. However, the Italian ruled the whole area of Abyssinia, Somaliland, and Eritrea until they were defeated in the Eastern African campaign in 1941. Emperor Haile Selassie returned to Addis Ababa in 1941, after five years in exile, and reclaimed his throne. Great Britain kept Eritrea under its rule until 1952 (Cassese 1995).

The debate regarding former Italian colonies and their future began in August 1945 at the Potsdam Conference (Germany) among Truman, Churchill, and Stalin. The issue of these colonies was forwarded to the next foreign ministers' meeting in London in September 1945 and then in the Paris Peace Conference on October 15, 1946. Italy was forced to renounce its title over the former colonies. Once Italy signed the peace treaty in 1947, the future of former Italian colonies shifted into the hands of the peace treaty. A commission was established to investigate the social, political, and economic situation of the region. But the parties did not agree on the report of the commission on September 15, 1948, in the London meeting. Thereby, the matter of former Italian colonies was passed to the United Nations General Assembly (Hail 1988, 19).

The issue was given to the First Committee of the UN, and the committee deliberated on the matter from April 6 to May 13, 1949. The committee came up with various proposals and recommendations. The plan called Bevin-Sforza formula was adopted, which was brought forward by British foreign secretary Ernest Bevin and Italian foreign minister Count Sforza. The plan was to divide Libya among three colonial powers of Britain, France, and Italy. Eritrea was to be divided between Anglo-Egyptian Sudan and Ethiopia. However, Eritrea and its supporter of an independent Eritrea rejected the Bevin-Sforza plan. Despite the strong opposition of the Eritrean leadership, the First Committee favored the Bevin-Sforza scheme of dividing Eritrea between Anglo-Egyptian lines and recommended it to the UN General Assembly. The Bevin-Sforza plan for Eritrea was defeated by Soviet Bloc in the United Nations, and another commission for Eritrea was proposed (Hail 1988, 20).

After Italy departed from the region, Great Britain campaigned for the division of Eritrea between Ethiopia and Sudan. Eritrean and other forces disagreed and opposed the division of Eritrea. They failed to reach an agreement; the case of Eritrea was referred to the United Nations. On November 21, 1949, UN resolution 269 (v) arranged a commission that was given the responsibility to gather proposals from different parties, governments, and regional organizations and submit its report to the UN by 1950. The commission came up with different reports and failed to agree with one conclusion. The UN General Assembly was not ready to hold a plebiscite to determine the wishes of the population of Eritrea (Cassese 1995, 220).

As the political crisis in the Horn of Africa worsened, it was also besieged by drought and famine. The political game of two big powers of the Soviet Union and America began to play in the region of the Horn, which comprises Ethiopia, Eritrea, Djibouti, and Somalia. America and the Soviet Union pushed for gaining more influence in the Horn of Africa. They were competing in North Africa, the Middle East, and the Indian Ocean for their political, economic, and strategic expansions (Hail 1988).

The Eritrean case was a complex one, as many parties had different interests relating to the region alongside the people of Eritrea. However, as the future of Eritrea was debated in the UN General Assembly in 1950 trying to find a solution for the matter, possibly considering the right to self-determination for Eritrea, but instead it ended up with resolution 390 A (V), federating Eritrea with Ethiopia. After a decade of the difficult and problematic federation, Emperor Haile Selassie eradicated the federal agreement and enforced his direct rule onto Eritrean territory (Hail 1988, 11).

The United Nations Commission for Eritrea

The new investigating commission for Eritrea was approved by the UN. The commission was to examine the best solution for the people of Eritrea, taking into account the wishes and welfare of inhabitants and various options and suggestions. Once again, despite the opposition of various members of the UN, including the Soviet Union, the Anglo-Egyptian proposal to federate Eritrea with Ethiopia was adopted. The Eritrean people were denied the right to self-determination. UN resolution 390 A (V) approved the Ethiopian-Eritrean federation on December 2, 1950, on the terms of full autonomy for the Eritrean government in all domestic affairs with definite limitations of the respective jurisdictions of both the Eritrean and Ethiopian governments, a demotic regime in Eritrea with all its requisites and safeguards, respect for human rights and fundamental liberties, and government of the people by the people.

The Ethiopian foreign minister assured the UN General Assembly that his country shall honor the terms and conditions of the federation. However, the federation's forced marriage resulted in a long and bloody war (Hail 1988, 21).

The Eritrean Federation with Ethiopia

The imposed federation of Eritrea with Ethiopia was designed to share the power between two regions in the hope of easing the tension and protecting their colonial interests. The federal powers were divided among the federal jurisdiction of Ethiopia, Eritrea, and the central government. Paragraph 3 of the UN resolution defined the power of the central governing body over the defense, foreign affairs, currency, and finance, which were to remain under the central government, and other regional issues will be dealt with by the regional authorities of the federation. The resolution also stated that Eritrea shall hold all those internal and external powers that are not vested in the federal government. Eritrea believed in the power-sharing machismo through the United Nations and accepted it fully with the hope that Ethiopia and Eritrea would find a way to discuss and resolve their differences through peaceful means and protect the interest of their people (Hail 1988, 22).

The division of power between Ethiopia and Eritrea was unique in such a federal system, both Eritrea and Ethiopia having their own legislative, executive, and judiciary for domestic matters. These three important governing bodies of the government were entrusted in paragraph 5 of the UN resolution 390 A (V). The Federal Act article 7 stated that the "citizens of Eritrea shall participate in the executive and judicial branches and shall be represented in the legislative branch of the Federal Government." Article 7 of the Federal Act also identified that an imperial federal council of five Eritrean and five Ethiopians would meet minimum once a year to discuss federal affairs, such as foreign and defense policy of the federation. The council was meant to be the bridge between the Eritrean government and Emperor Haile Selassie (Hail 1988, 23).

The UN General Assembly granted the responsibility to its commissioner to implement the federal rules defined under paragraphs 12, 13, and 15 of the federal resolution. On December 14, 1950, Dr. Eduardo Anze Matienzo was given the mandate as UN commissioner in Eritrea. The commissioner and his team arrived in Asmara on February 9, 1951. The first thing was to draft the Constitution of Eritrea according to the federation rules adopted by the UN General Assembly. He met various local leadership and discussed the federal union with Ethiopia. He received support and also opposition from the local leaders, but his mission to draft the constitution was hindered by Ethiopian foreign minister Aklilu Habte-Wold who pushed for more central rule and jurisdiction favoring Ethiopia. This was undermining the hard work of the commissioner to establish Eritrea as a sound autonomous region. The principal job of the commissioner was to safeguard the full autonomy of Eritrea in the federal system according to the mandate he was given by the United Nations (Hail 1988, 24–25).

The commissioner submitted his final draft of the Federal Act and the Eritrean Constitution to the Ethiopian government for approval on April 25, 1952. The British administration in Eritrea administered the imposed election and chose sixty-eight members of the Eritrean Assembly through people, dividing the assembly seats on a religious basis—thirty-four for Christian and thirty-four for Muslim—and shaped the government of Eritrea in the same manner. According to the British plan for Eritrea, Tedla Bairu, the leader of the Unionist Party, was chosen as the president of the Eritrean Assembly and the Eritrean Muslim League (EML) leader, Ali Mohammad Mussa Radi, became the vice president. As arranged, the British and Ethiopian supporters formed the government and immediately passed the Federal Act and the Constitution of Eritrea on July 10, 1952. The federation of Eritrea with Ethiopia was the plan of the United States and Great Britain, but they pushed forward this plan through the United Nations. As the federation was sponsored by the United Nations, the people of Eritrea were hopeful that the UN would safeguard the rules of the federation; but unfortunately, their hopes began to fade away as soon as it came to the implementation of the federal system in the region. When Ethiopia violated the federal constitution and extended its jurisdiction into Eritrean territory, the chief executive of Eritrea, Tedla Bairu, protested against Ethiopian actions, but he was replaced by the emperor's vice president, Asfaha Wolde-Michael (Hail 1988).

The Eritrean Right to Self-Determination

Ethiopia never accepted Eritrean as a nation or that they have the right to self-determination. For over the years, Ethiopia constantly insisted that Eritrea is an integral part of Ethiopia and Eritrean people will never be allowed to break away from Ethiopian territory. The government and Ethiopian rulers argued that Eritrea had always been, one way or the other, part of Ethiopia. Their claims were based on the history of Eritrean territory during the Italian conquest and beyond that. The area had been under the Kingdom of Aksum and Abyssinia control since the first century BCE. In its heydays, the kingdom was expanded through present Eritrea, western Yemen, southern Saudi Arabia, and Sudan (Cassese 1995).

Ethiopia argued that there had never been an Eritrean nation and that the Eritrean territory was part of Ethiopia without any dispute until the Italian conquest in that part of Africa. The concept of Eritrean as a nation was brought forward by Italians who colonized the region. Even though the territory was part of Ethiopia, the Eritrean population was given the right to exercise their will for the united country in 1952. The Eritrean Assembly unanimously voted for the union of Ethiopia and recognized the importance of great united Ethiopia. Moreover, the Eritrean people have used their right to self-determination through their assembly and representatives for the unification of the motherland. Thereby, they will no longer hold the right to invoke or claim self-determination for Eritrean people and accept the territorial integrity of Ethiopia (Cassese 1995).

On the other hand, Eritreans had always maintained their separate identity and expressed a will for the right of self-determination. They argued that their right to self-determination must be respected under the internationally recognized rules and Ethiopia should not be allowed to keep denying their right as a nation. The Eritrean claim of self-determination was based on the following grounds:

The precolonial history of the region showed no evidence that there had been a country that included both Ethiopia and Eritrea as a one-nation state.

The act of the Ethiopian federation in 1952 was imposed on Eritrean people against their will. There were no measures involved to determine the wishes of Eritrean people like other cases—for example, UN actions in Togoland and the Southern Cameroon in 1961.

The forcible annexation of Eritrea by Ethiopia in 1952 showed that Ethiopia was in complete denial of accepting the right of the Eritrean population (Cassese 1995, 221).

Eritrean people considered the federation was designed to occupy their homeland, but at the same time, they were not in the position to resist the imposed idea of big powers immediately. However, within a few years, a series of independence movants emerged in Eritrea. The Eritrean Liberation Front (ELF) was founded in 1961, followed by the Eritrean People's Liberation Front (EPLF) in 1970. These organizations started an armed struggle against Ethiopian forces. The ELF and EPLF had political differences, but their aim was the same—both fought for an independent Eritrea. Ethiopian authorities placed the region under direct army administration, but guerrilla warfare continued between Ethiopian and Eritrean freedom fighters (Hannum 1996).

After a long war for freedom of Eritrea, on May 29, 1991, the secretary-general of the Eritrean People's Liberation Front (EPLF), Isaias Afwerki, announced the Provisional Government of Eritrea and called on United Nations to take the responsibility for a free and fair referendum on the demand of Eritrean people for the right to self-determination. On the other hand, the Ethiopian regime of Mengistu

Haile Mariam lost the support of the Soviet Union, and America and Great Britain also changed their policy toward Eritrea's right to self-determination. They started to recognize the Eritrean people's right to decide their future. They even became parties into the negation to end the conflict and allow the Eritrean people to choose their destiny through a referendum under the supervision of the United Nations. The referendum was held on April 23 and 25, 1993, and a new state emerged on the map of the world.

South Sudan

The flag of South Sudan, a new country, was raised in its capital, Juba, on July 9, 2011. The ceremony was full of joy, and people waved their small flags, sang, and danced. Many world leaders attended the celebrations of the new country alongside the people of South Sudan. The people of South Sudan achieved their independence after a long struggle and a civil war that took the life of two and a half million people. People cheered and cried for those they had lost in their long journey to freedom. One thousand and two hundred kilometers away from the northern capital of Khartoum, the nationalists mourned for losing the South as they fought against Egypt-European colonial powers side by side and gained their freedom in 1956. The dream of a united Sudan faded away during decades of civil wars and bloodshed and ultimately died in January 2011 when the south voted for an independent South Sudan (Copnall 2014).

The region came under British influence after the Turk and Mahdist era. Anglo-Egyptian administrations ruled Sudan from one corner to another from 1899 to 1956. This period of rule is known as Anglo-Egyptian Condominium—the joint government of the region. The governors-general were appointed and began to operate from the capital of Khartoum. All governors-general of the region were under a certain degree of supervision by the British foreign office in Cairo (Daly 1991). Although, as the colonial forces attempted to bring all areas of Sudan under their firm control, the hostility increased, especially in the South. Because the South was different from the North, the British used different methods to control the population. The South and the North were treated as two different entities until 1947. Despite the joint governing system, the British had the upper hand in most decision-making and in ruling the territory. The occupying forces were confronted with some resistance in the south, but soon they overcame these small group attacks.

Northern Sudan followed the Arab culture and Islamic way of life, and the South practiced Christianity and their local religion and African traditions (Copnall 2014). Southern people considered themselves as African in their way of life, and the Northern population recognized themselves as Arabs and traced their roots to the Middle East. These differences of Sudan had always existed throughout its history, and the concept of two Sudans continued until it became two states. In 1922, the British even introduced travel documents between two parts of Sudan. Both parts also used a different set of customs and laws that were according to their traditions and culture. Northern Sudan became the headquarters of all colonialists; therefore, the area had received some benefits from the governing authorities. At least Khartoum and its surrounding parts were developed to some extent, but the rest of the region remained underdeveloped (Copnall 2014).

The Egyptian Free Officers Movement of 1952 did not only end the long-running dynastic Egyptian monarchy but also changed the game for colonialism in Egypt. It became more difficult for the British forces to continue their colonial bases in the region. The period is known as the era of decolonization of Africa and other parts of the world. Alongside many other states, Sudan emerged as an independent country on January 1, 1956. Sudan did not adopt a clear path of the governing system, and the crucial historical issues of the South and North were not addressed in the constitution of 1956. The Arab-led government of Sudan never took the South seriously. Southern leaders learned that the Khartoum was reluctant to meet their demands; thereby, war erupted between North and South, which ended with the Addis Ababa Agreement in 1972. In the agreement, an autonomous status was granted to the South with a promise of a referendum to determine the future of Southern people (Copnall 2014).

The British idea of South becoming part of Northern Sudan did not go down well in the South, and before the independence of Sudan, the war began between North and South Sudan in August 1955. The war between South and North was inevitable, as the South considered Northern advances in their land to be the replacement of British colonial power with an Islamic North that had a deep-rooted conflict for a century. The South first demanded greater autonomy and a federal system of government, but when the conflict deepened and the North pushed for forceful integration, the Southern political call changed for a separate and independent South Sudan. The political situation changed as the army took over just after two years of independence. Military rulers continued to ignore the South and pursued their path to Islamization and Arabization, disregarding the Christian and African beliefs and culture of the Southern people (Deng 1995).

There was a little bit of hope after independence and during the 1957 election that North and South might find a way forward, but the situation deteriorated when the army took over in 1958. The centralization, Islamization, and Arabization of Sudan increased under General Ibrahim Abboud during his six-year rule in Sudan (Johnson 2003). The army's centralizing actions met with strong opposition especially from the South, and thereby a brutal operation began in the South. During 1960–1062, torture, burning down entire villages, and mass killing of civilians were carried out by the army. Most leaders of the South went underground or left the country. The exile leaders of South Sudan sustained their struggle against Khartoum's repression and organized guerrilla attacks on the government forces in various parts of the country. The exile movement later emerged as the Sudan African Nationalist Union (SANU). However, the Anya Nya was not well-organized or had the means and support from outside to engage the Sudani army in strong guerilla warfare. Their weapons were stolen from the police forces or gained from the deserting South Sudani forces. The Anya Nya only gained some military training and weapons after 1964. This was a chaotic time for Sudan. General Ibrahim Abboud was overthrown, and the international policy began to change about Sudan's conflict, although the right to self-determination for South Sudan was not getting much support from the neighboring African countries, which were the newly emerging states from the European colonization (Johnson 2003).

General Abboud's departure in 1964 brought back civilian rule in Sudan. All parties were called to participate in the election and find a peaceful solution for the South Sudan conflict. Some South Sudan leaders agreed to take part in the election and continue their campaign for a federal system for the country within, but some leaders of SANU didn't agree. The SANU broke apart. William Deng returned to Sudan to take part in the new government and work for a federal governing system in Sudan. Jaden and Joseph Oduho stayed outside the country as the leaders of SANU and continued advocacy for an independent South Sudan. Saturnino Lohure engaged himself with the guerilla army until he was killed by the Ugandan army in 1967. The return of William Deng to democratic politics left SANU weakened and divided. In exile, factional differences between Jaden and Oduho deepened at first, but later they came together under the umbrella of a new name, the Azania Liberation Front in 1965, based in Kampala (Johnson 2003).

The forced assimilation policy of the government was met with strong opposition from the South, and by the 1960s, the country was engulfed by a full civil war that led to the popular uprising against the military regime and for the overthrow of the government in 1964. As democracy returned to the country, the oppressive policy toward the South was halted for a little while, but the differences of parties and tribes turned into a cycle of violence that led to another military coup of Gaafar Mohamed el-Nimeiri in 1969. When the military took over again this time, the Nimeiri junta tried to bring Southern leaders on board. The negation began between the government and the Southern Sudan Liberation Movement (SSLM). The Addis Ababa Agreement in 1972 brought forward new hope for a peaceful and united Sudan. However, some groups fighting for a separate South Sudan were reluctant to give up their struggle, as they didn't trust the Khartoum government. But the agreement was a real chance for peace in Sudan; thereby, all parties agreed. An autonomous South Sudan and federal governing system for the country was negotiated and agreed. The peace process began, but the most difficult and delicate task was the two opposing security forces to handle. Neither the Anya Nya guerilla forces wanted to change their unit nor the central government forces were willing to join their group in their region. They were enemy forces fighting against each other for a long time, and harmonizing them was not an easy job, and some of the low-ranking guerillas were even not included in the army. Some of the Anya Nya members were integrated into the police force, and many refused to join the government forces and left the country (Johnson 2003).

After granting the South autonomy, the Nimeiri government came under pressure from the Muslim Brotherhood and other radical forces of the North. It was not easy for Nimeiri to sideline his opponents, as he came to power through their support, especially as he was supported by the Muslim Brotherhood. He thought he could first defuse the tension between the South and North and then go after religious fanatics (Deng 1995). However, the Nimeiri regime did the opposite of what was expected from the Khartoum. The military regime of Nimeiri extended its full control to the South. He imposed Sharia law and tried to establish an Islamic state. The South strongly opposed the authoritarian actions of the central government and the concept of an Islamic state of Sudan. Thereafter, the military junta unilaterally renounced the Addis Ababa Agreement, which was the breaking point of political engagement between the South and the North. The opposing leaders of the Nimeiri regime formed the Sudan People's Liberation Movement (SPLM) and also formed a military wing of this organization, the Sudan People's Liberation Army (SPLA). The Sudan People's Liberation Movement aimed to establish a secular and democratic Sudan (Deng 1995).

Hostility intensified with a popular revolt known as intifada, which led Nimeiri's political demise in 1985. The following governments failed to bring the SPLM and SPLA to any kind of settlement or meaningful dialogues. On the other hand, Sharia triggered the fierce debate that meant the Islamization and Arabization of Sudan despite the opposition of other groups. Sharia was one of the greatest obstacles for any stability and peaceful solution to the conflict. In June 1989, the Islamic group in the army took over under the leadership of Brigadier Omar Hassan Ahmad al-Bashir. These army officers with their leader, Bashir, pushed for more Islamic Sharia laws, which widened the gap further between South and North (Deng 1995).

It seems SPLM–SPLA leaders concluded that fighting for justice, democracy, and equality might gain more support and sympathy within Africa and beyond than calling for secession. They thought working within the framework of Sudan could provide more chances to cooperate with other secular forces in building a democratic and secular Sudan. Despite the widening gaps between South and North, the prospect of working together for a democratic and secular Sudan was welcomed by some Northern political parties. These Northern political groups were already opposing the Islamic and Sharia laws. Supporting the idea of a united and democratic Sudan, these elements reached an agreement with SPLM–SPLA and made an alliance called National Democratic Alliance (NDA) (Deng 1995). The attempt of the National Democratic Alliance to bring the government into some kind of understanding failed, and armed conflict resumed between government and NDA forces (Deng 1995).

The Second Civil War began in 1983 led by John Garang, the leader of Sudan People's Liberation Army. The movement was for reform and equal rights for all Sudan people. He believed that Sudan could stay united if there was a reformed and just government addressing the issues of all people. John Garang's idea of a united Sudan fell on deaf ears, as Khartoum continued to renege on its promises, and his sudden death buried the last strong voice from the South for one Sudan with him. On January 9, 2005, a Comprehensive Peace Agreement between Khartoum and the Sudan People's Liberation Movement ended the Second Civil War of Sudan. They also agreed on a referendum to determine South Sudan's future. The struggle for an independent South Sudan reached its destiny on January 9, 2011 (Copnall 2014).

South Sudan has a population of around ten million, which is a major ethnic group. The region bordered Arab-Muslim Sudan on the north, Chad on the west, Zaire and Uganda on the south, and Kenya and Ethiopia on the east. South Sudan achieved independence on July 9, 2011, through a referendum that ended one of the longest-running civil war in African history.

South Sudan in Context

To understand the dimension and objectives of the self-determination struggle of the people of South Sudan, one has to go through a brief history of the region. Before the Turko-Egyptian incursion of 1821, Sudan was loosely ruled by kings and a tribal system, and there were no clear territorial boundaries during that period. Egyptians ruled the region for decades, but they were not able to bring the whole of Sudan under their control, especially the areas of South Sudan.

European powers rapidly conquered Africa in the nineteenth century, the period called the Scramble for Africa. The powers involved in this scramble were France, Britain, Germany, Italy, Spain, Portugal, and Belgium. Later in 1892, the Belgians started to advance in the region, capturing present Zaire, Equatoria up to Mongalla, making them part of Belgian Congo. On the other side, French forces captured a large part of South Sudan, Bahr el Ghazal up to Fashoda, and established control over the area. The French ambition was to keep South Sudan within its West African colonies but had to leave the region over the Fashoda conflict with Britain (Teny-Dhurgon 1995).

Sudan was recaptured by joint forces of Britain and Egypt in 1898, and they arrived on an administrative agreement that was to run the business of the region within their sharing interests. The British and French reached an agreement that made the French forces pull out from South Sudan, handing over control to the British authorities. Due to the major historical, political, and cultural differences between South and Northern Sudan, the British adopted two separate administrative systems to run both regions (Teny-Dhurgon 1995).

The British and Egyptians advocated that South and North Sudan should stay under the rule of Khartoum at the Khartoum Conference in 1946, and then the last nail was hammered down into the coffin of South Sudan in 1948 when the British handed over the ruling keys to Khartoum. Thirteen people were chosen by the British and Khartoum in the Juba Conference to represent South Sudan in the assembly of a new master. Since that decision, South Sudanese regarded themselves as "internally colonized people" (Teny-Dhurgon 1995).

While Sudan was preparing to gain freedom from the British and Egyptians in 1956, the leaders of South Sudan accused Khartoum of not only following a federal system for the country but also imposing an Arabic and Islamic culture on them. When South Sudan learned that the Sudanese government was not going to respect their pledge for autonomy, the armed conflict erupted in 1955 between Anya Nya guerrilla and the government of Sudan. The ceasefire only took place after the Addis Ababa peace agreement of 1972 (BBC 2013).

There was another wave of civil war in 1983, following the breakdown of the 1972 Addis Ababa peace pact. The human loss reached up to over two million during armed conflict, more than four million people were displaced, and around six hundred thousand people fled the country. Thereby, there were many attempts taken by neighboring countries and the UN to bring both parties to a table for peace, which failed. Eventually, a peace agreement eased the conflict in 2005, which assured regional autonomy to South Sudan (UNMIS 2004).

On July 20, 2002, both parties agreed on the Machakos Protocol to set the governing structures and process the right of self-determination of South Sudan. There were also more recommendations made to the UN. In 2004, UN resolution 1547 (2004) Advance Mission in Sudan (UNAMIS) was maintained to continue the dialogue and peace process in the region. The turning point of Sudan's history arrived on January 9, 2005, when both parties signed the Nairobi Comprehensive Peace Agreement (CPA), which included power-sharing, security, and autonomy for the South (UNAMIS 2004).

The UNAMIS mission was focused on the commitments of deployment of peacekeeping forces in the disputed areas and preparation for the referendum in 2011 that will give South Sudan to choose its fate. The referendum to determine the fate of South Sudan was held according to the schedule in January 2011. People of South Sudan voted for independence with the overwhelming majority of 98.83 percent. The UN secretary-general said that the UNAMIS had achieved its aims and thanked all international partners for their efforts to make it happen (UNAMIS 2004).

Western Sahara

The dispute of Western Sahara runs throughout its history. The region, which is a huge barren land extending to the area of 102,700 square miles, has been ruled by various forces alongside the native Sahrawi people. Western Sahara is one of the long-disputed areas in North Africa. Spain declared control on the territory in 1884, which was the time of the division of Africa by European powers. Later in 1958, while decolonization of Africa began, Spain decided to turn Western Sahara to an autonomous province. On the other hand, Morocco's ambition for greater territory began as soon as it gained its freedom from France and Spain in 1965. The Moroccans believed that all Spanish-controlled areas belonged to them, but the claim of Morocco was met with opposing parties of Mauritania, Algeria, and native Sahrawi (Hodges 1983).

Since then, the area turned into a war zone mainly between Western Saharan and Moroccan forces. The indigenous people of Western Sahara had rejected the Moroccan claim on their homeland

and began fighting for their separate identity as Sahrawi people. They proclaimed their ethnicity as Sahrawi who were inhabitants of that region for centuries and that they would never become Moroccan or Mauritanian. Western Saharan people considered their case as one of those unfinished decolonization processes like many others around the world, and it seemed the international community agreed with them and promoted their right to self-determination. Sahrawi people had been struggling for the same right offered to other European colonies. The leaders of the native people defined their struggle as for self-determination, meaning the democratic right to choose their future for their homeland (Zunes and Mundy 2010).

Concerning the claims of Morocco and Mauritania, the UN General Assembly passed a resolution in 1975 calling for a referendum in Western Sahara. The United Nations passed the resolution for a referendum and recognized the right to the people of Western Sahara to decide their future, and the Spanish government also stood for the self-determination of the people of the region and supported the proposal for a referendum. In 1975, the International Court of Justice also accepted the historical relationship of the region with the state's concern and granted the legal right to the local people to decide their free will whether they want to be part of Mauritania, Morocco, or an independent state. These two neighboring countries invaded the vast desert land of Western Sahara in 1975 on the departure of Spain from the area. When they were refused their birth rights, the reaction was clear to them. The liberation movement of Western Sahara demanded the withdrawal of both occupying states from the territory (Cassese 1995).

Eventually, Mauritania withdrew in 1979, and Morocco took control of Western Sahara. Since then, Polisario had been gaining support from the member states of the United Nations and enjoyed the official recognition of the African Union. Despite the clear support from the International Court of Justice, the United Nations, and the African Union, the referendum plan has been delayed and compromised for decades. There have been various resolutions for a referendum in the United Nations, peace plan, agreement, ceasefire negotiations in London, Lisbon, and Houston, but unfortunately, the long-running case of Western Sahara is still waiting to be resolved.

Historical Background of Western Sahara

It is believed that during the first millennium BC people tended to move southward. The Berbers nomadic people arrived in the territory from the north. The earliest Berbers who entered the Sahara were Sanhaja, one of the toughest main Berber groups that dominated the area. Africa was the first continent that the Muslim faith reached in the seventh century. It gained power when Almoravids conquered the territory. In 1062, Abdullah ibn Yasin founded Marrakech City as the capital of the region and consolidated his power over a vast area. However, the power game kept changing throughout the years. Various dynastic rulers gained a different degree of control over the territory (Jensen 2005).

Arab Bedouin tribes arrived in the region in the eleventh century, and they advanced into Western Sahara. Despite the resistance of native people of Sahara, an invading tribe called Beni Hasan managed to develop a stronghold on the territory for a long time. The nomadic Sahrawi people were always on the move for the search of water and pastures for their animals. They were known as cloud followers or the children of the clouds. They followed clouds for thousands of miles in the hope of rainfall. Their roaming had no borders except the Atlantic coastline. These tribes moved freely into a vast area of land that now covers three countries of Algeria, Morocco, and Mauritania. They fiercely resisted outsiders in their territory, and even the Europeans had very little influence in the hostile region (Jensen 2005, 23).

In 1884, Europeans arrived in the region. Spain attempted to maintain a citadel in Western Sahara in 1476 and 1517, but without success. The Spanish reinforced their presence on the coast of Western Sahara, which was followed by the French and English. They took positions in different parts of the region and extended their control over hundreds of miles. Sahrawi resistance continued, and they attacked the Spanish fort. However, later they reached an agreement with Shaikh Ould Laroussi, the chief of the Oulad Delim tribe. The tribal leader believed that it was better to trade with the Spanish than fight with them. Many other tribal groups did not agree with the Oulad Delim agreement, and the battle went on in many parts of Sahara with Spanish and other occupying forces (Jensen 2005).

In 1900, France and Spain agreed to respect each other's possessions in the region. Later in 1904, the European occupying powers signed the Morocco convention in Paris demarcating some of their territories in the northern borders. The treaty of 1912 regarding Morocco, signed by France and Spain, further defined their possessions in the area. However, in various parts of Morocco and Western Sahara, local tribes continued their fight against French and Spanish forces. During the Moroccan campaign for independence in 1956, Sahrawi and Moroccan forces fought against Spanish rule (Besenyo 2009).

Spanish rule began to decline during the1970s, and by 1975, the colonial power knew that it was losing the game in Africa. Thereby, Spain decided to depart from Western Sahara. Before leaving the territory, the case of Western Sahara was forwarded to the International Court of Justice for an advisory opinion regarding its and the Sahrawi people's future. The Spanish role was going to end by 1976. On the one hand, Mauritania and Morocco had been claiming Western Sahara; and on the other hand, the Sahrawi National Liberation Movement was struggling for the self-determination of the region, naming it Sahrawi Arab Democratic Republic (Jensen 2005).

On the departure of Spain from Western Sahara, the Polisario intensified their struggle for freedom against Morocco and Mauritania. The Moroccan army maintained its possession over a vast area by building a two-thousand-kilometer defensive wall, but Mauritania gave up its claim on the territory. The war continued between Morocco's and Polisario's freedom fighters. The battle for Western Sahara reached the UN Security Council. During 1990–1991, the UN planned a settlement for the Western Saharan people, which meant they would have to decide their future by a referendum, voting either for independence or integration with Morocco. While the United Nations planned for a settlement taking place, both parties agreed to a cease-fire, but they disagreed on who should be allowed to vote for the referendum (Jensen 2005).

The Conflict and Solutions

During the 1960s, Western Sahara made its way to the international arena through various UN General Assembly resolutions. The United Nations supported the decolonization of the region and the right of self-determination of Saharan people. The territory was also claimed by Morocco and Mauritania. Despite the UN resolutions for decolonization, the Spanish presence continued in Western Sahara until 1974. Although the Spanish rulers were facing a rebellion in the territory from native Sahrawi, which was suppressed during the1970s, after three years, a new movement of Polisario Front emerged in Western Sahara demanding the right of self-determination for the region (Zunes and Mundy 2010).

In 1974, Spain planned to hold a referendum in Western Sahara with a year to determine the will of Sahrawi people. Morocco disagreed with the Spanish plan, fearing that Western Sahara might vote for a separate state, asking for an opinion from the International Court of Justice. Despite the strong position of Morocco on the international polity, the International Court supported the right of native Sahrawi people. The judgment of the court was published on October 16, 1975. The decision of the court was clear regarding Morocco's historical possession on the territory. However, the court accepted the right of native Sahrawi people over their homeland, and the Moroccan claim was rejected by the International Court. Morocco's king Hassan II was appalled by the judgment of the court and announced a civilian march over Western Sahara known as Green March, asserting that the territory was an integral part of Morocco (Zunes and Mundy 2010).

In Spain, the illness of General Franco weakened the Spanish position of support for Western Sahara and was not able to put forward a clear plan for the region. Meanwhile, Morocco was gaining the support of the United States and France in the United Nations. The Spanish presence in Western Sahara came under immense pressure from various sides. The Green March and Moroccan army advance on eastern Saguia el-Hamra in October made it difficult for Spain to sustain its presence in the region. Thereby, the Spanish authorities decided to exit quietly from the territory, leaving the fate of Western Sahrawi people in the hands of Morocco and Mauritania. The Madrid Tripartite Accord of November 14, 1975, made Spain's way out from the region, which was signed by Spain, Morocco, and Mauritania. The agreement among these three countries about Western Sahara was a brazen denial of the right of self-determination of Sahrawi people who should have a right to be included in any decision regarding their homeland. The Spanish departed from its former colony followed by the invasion of Morocco and Mauritanian forces. The mounting army attacks pushed half of the Sahrawi population into the Algerian area of Tindouf (Zunes and Mundy 2010).

The Sahrawi liberation movement known as Polisario worked as a government in exile for Western Sahara and established the Sahrawi Arab Democratic Republic (SADR) on February 27, 1976, and began a new wave of guerrilla warfare against Morocco and Mauritania. The Polisario forces first intensified their attacks against Mauritania, which had a far weaker army than Morocco. The guerrilla attacks of Polisario managed to reach the capital, Nouakchott, destabilizing the whole country. The Polisario attacks were also reaching inside Morocco, sending a clear message to Mauritania that they could fight this war against both occupying countries. Mauritania realized that the war for Western Sahara could be costly for the whole country and decided to give up its claim over the region. Mauritania signed the peace agreement on August 5, 1979, recognizing the right of the Sahrawi in their homeland (Zunes and Mundy 2010).

As soon as Mauritanian forces pulled out from the Polisario area, Moroccan king Hassan II seized the occasion and sent his forces into the former Mauritanian-occupied areas of Western Sahara. The Moroccan invasion of this new frontier outraged the Polisario movement for freedom, and they increased their guerrilla attacks against the Moroccan army in various parts of the country. Morocco maintained its presence by constructing a long sand wall (the Moroccan Wall) extending around 2,700 km. into Western Sahara. These defensive walls were built to control the movements of Polisario in the territory. These walls and Moroccan strategies of barring Polisario from the area made it difficult for the guerrilla forces to fight an effective war against Morocco's occupation in their territories. Neither Polisario nor Morocco was in a position to win the war for Western Sahara, so they decided to use other options.

When the United Nations secretary-general initiated a peace mission in 1988, with the support of the Organization of African Unity (OAU), both parties in Morocco and Polisario agreed to cooperate with negotiations. Cooperating and agreeing with the UN mission did not mean that the Sahrawi or the Moroccans were giving up their positions in some ways, but they began a new chapter to win Western Sahara by a democratic means of the referendum. The cease-fire of 1991 was the result of the UN and OAU's hard work, convincing both parties that there was no solution to this conflict through smoking guns. The most difficult challenge for the UN mission was to determine who had the right to vote for the suggested referendum. The Polisario demand was to use the Spanish census of 1974 for the right to vote for the referendum, but Rabat argued that the census carried out by the Spanish was incomplete, and Morocco sought to include those who were moved into Western Sahara by Rabat to gain support in the case of a referendum. Polisario rejected the Moroccan plan to include those who were pushed into their homeland later by Rabat (Zunes and Mundy 2010).

However, the process of checking thousands of applications for voters began in 1994 but ended in 1996 without getting anywhere. Thereafter, in 1997, UN secretary-general Kofi Annan took one step forward by giving former US secretary of state James Baker the responsibility to find a solution for the Western Saharan conflict. James Baker reopened the negotiations between Morocco and Polisario and was pleased to find that both parties were still in favor of holding the referendum to determine the fate of the territory. The registration of the voters resumed, and it was completed after two years, but before the matter could go further for a referendum, King Hassan of Morocco died. The successor of King Hassan, his son Mohammed VI, was not keen to hold a referendum in Western Sahara. It was the time when East Timor decided to break away from Indonesia through a referendum, which resulted in 78 percent of people voting for an independent East Timor. The referendum result of East Timor was alarming to Morocco that the Rabat might lose the referendum in Western Sahara too. Thereby, Rabat did not only stop cooperating with the UN plan for a referendum but also began to grab more land from Western Sahara (Zunes and Mundy 2010).

From 2000 to 2004, James Baker continued his mission for a peaceful settlement between Morocco and the Sahrawi people. Baker brought forward two new proposals to solve Western Sahara's conflict through peaceful means. The third way of Baker's plan for a settlement between independence and integration was approved by both sides. According to this agreement, Western Sahara was given a considerable autonomy of self-government and the right to have a referendum after five years for the final decision. By 2002, the Security Council suggested that it would agree with any settlement plan that gave the right of self-determination to Western Sahara (Zunes and Mundy 2010, 32).

A revised plan called Peace Plan came into being in 2003. The proposal comprised more autonomy for Western Sahara under Moroccan sovereignty during a four-year time, and then it would be followed by a referendum. The final status of the region would be determined through a vote on independence, integration, or the continued autonomous position of Western Sahara. The Security Council agreed with the peace plan alongside Polisario, Algeria, and Morocco. Baker strongly recommended the peace plan to the Security Council and asked for a tangible framework to achieve a solution for the long-running conflict, but he was very disappointed by Rabat's noncooperative behavior and resigned in 2004, saying he had done whatever he could (Zunes and Mundy 2010, 33).

Sustaining the Cease-Fire

The cease-fire has been holding in Western Sahara since the agreement of 1991. However, there have been some violations in 2000, and Polisario reminded the UN to keep its promise of a referendum for self-determination and threatened that if the UN were unable to conduct the promised referendum, then they would resume their armed struggle against Rabat. The situation intensified, and Polisario began to mobilize the armed forces for a looming war, and the cease-fire came to a breaking point. Algeria intervened, preventing the smoking guns between Morocco and Polisario armed forces. Since then, despite the increasing tension between Rabat and Polisario, the cease-fire has been holding on, and UN representatives for peace and dialogue have been pushing both parties to find a peaceful solution and avoid the destructive armed conflict (Zunes and Mundy 2010).

Morocco put forward a proposal of autonomy in 2007 stating that any other options might lead to another war, suggesting that the peaceful means might take time to reach the destination but must be respected with patience, but Polisario declared it as another ploy for delaying and buying time from Rabat. Sahrawi people had been patient for decades with UN representatives coming and going. As the promises and dateline kept changing for the referendum, the Polisario began to contemplate resuming the armed struggle rather than waiting for the world to respond to their long-running demand for self-determination. The majority of Western Sahrawi believe that the Moroccan regime can only understand the language of guns, but the leadership of Western Saharan people think that peaceful and democratic means are still valid and can work (Zunes and Mundy 2010).

They also believe that the time is not right for resuming the armed struggle. Armed conflict with Morocco will open a door for Moroccan forces to indiscriminately target the Sahrawi populations and completely ignore the pressure from their supporting countries and the UN. Polisario-supporting countries under the UN notion for a referendum in Western Sahara have been struggling to gain the full backing of the United States and France; these two big powers maintained some special relationships with Rabat. The United States and France had developed these friendly ties with Morocco during the 1970 and 1980s.

However, the refugee nation of Western Sahara is losing patience, as the plan of the referendum keeps extending for years and years. If the situation does not improve, then it may lead to a flash point, meaning more destruction and human loss that can be avoided by a peaceful solution to the conflict. During the cease-fire, Polisario continued to train its forces and recruit newcomers who were willing to fight for their rights. Both sides are watching each other's army movements closely and are ready for any action. Polisario has gained much more manpower and weapons during all these years of peace talks and is in a better position for any armed conflict with Morocco if their demands are not met with peaceful means. Although the Sahrawi forces are not in a position to defeat Rabat by a full-fledged war, they would put great pressure on Rabat by their guerrilla warfare if the war is resumed (Zunes and Mundy 2010).

The idea of a referendum for Western Sahara seems to be like a desert mirage, especially for the Sahrawi who keep dreaming of their own country and way of life. The referendum mirage of Sahrawi people stays away over the desert dunes of Sahara despite looking very close to them. The challenging factors for the UN and the supporting countries of Saharan people are who are real Sahrawi and who has the right to vote in a referendum for self-determination. The UN Security Council has failed in its mission to conduct the referendum that was approved by all parties involved in the conflict. Since then, Morocco has changed its plan and political strategies at times, and the Western Sahara conflict seems to be heading toward an unknown territory.

Bangladesh

Bangladesh comprised of eastern regions of divided Bengal. Despite being quite a new country, the land of Bangladesh has a long history spanning over four thousand years. In its early time, it was also known as Banga and was ruled by various groups; but in modern history, it was part of India and called East Bengal. In the scheme of dividing India and creating Pakistan on religious grounds, this part of Bengal was incorporated into Pakistan; and for a while, it was known as East Pakistan. After twenty-four years with the newborn country, Bengalis realized that Pakistan was not a country for them or Muslims; it turned out to be a country for a military junta. After a bloody war with its west wing, Bangladesh became an independent country in 1971.

The early history of Bengal can be traced back to the seventh century BC. It is believed that the word *Bengal* came from the Dravidian tribes who settled in the region around 1000 BC. The ancient region of Bengal had seen various kingdoms and dynasties throughout its long history. In the Gupta Empire around 300–600 CE, the inhabitants of Bengal spoke Sanskrit. It is believed that later during 1000 AD, the Bengali language evolved, and today it's the seventh most spoken language with 250 million speakers.

Bengal played an important role in the Indian subcontinent from its early history to the end of the British Empire in 1947. According to *Mahabharata*, the region was first unified by the Nanda dynasty during 7 BC. The Buddhist Pala Empire ruled the area during 750–1120, which consolidated its power all over Bengal. They built temples, supported the work of art, and created institutions for learning. The Pala dynasty was replaced by the Sena dynasty, which was known as Kannada kings. Unlike their predecessors, the Sena dynasty was Hindu and they worked on Hinduism and Sanskrit literature. The son of Ballala, the philosopher king Lakshmanasena, expanded his reign over Bihar, Assam, and Odisha during the twelfth century. He was one of the greatest kings of his time who was later defeated by Turkic Muslim invaders (Malley 1908).

Bengal was ruled by the Ilyas Shahi dynasty during 1342–1487, which was replaced by the Ganesha dynasty for a while, and then again, the Shahi dynasty took control back from 1494 to 1538. Islam arrived later through the invading forces. In the process of converting people to Islam, they built mosques and madrassas. The region came under the Mughal Empire in 1526. When the Mughal Empire began to decline during the 1700s, Bengal became an autonomous region under the nawabs of Bengal until the Battle of Plassey on June 23, 1757, where the British defeated the forces of the nawab of Bengal and took over control of the Bengal region. This was the beginning of the British Raj over the Indian subcontinent (Ahmed 2004).

The Great British Empire began to crumble after the Second World War, and many states emerged from its ruins in Asia and Africa. With the changing dynamics of post–world war polity, the independence of India became inevitable; however, to safeguard its geostrategic interests in the region, it became imperative for the British to create a client state out of India. Using the two-nation theory, India was divided and the religious state of Pakistan was created in 1947. Bengal was divided, and its eastern parts were incorporated into the new state as East Pakistan. Punjab-dominated western regions were named West Pakistan. The incorporation of East Bengal into the religious state was a short-lived affair. After a bloody civil war, East Pakistan became modern Bangladesh in 1971 (Ahmed 2004).

After the British administration decided to divide India in the name of Hindu and Muslim beliefs, they selected the Muslim League party for demanding the creation of Pakistan. The Muslim League was created in 1906 by people having a long-term relationship with the colonial administration. The majority of Muslim League leaders were those who had been on the payroll of the East India Company. During the 1930s, Mr. Mohammed Ali Jinnah, a trusted protégé of the colonial administration, was chosen to lead the pro-British party in India. On August 17, 1936, he arranged a meeting in Kolkata with Bengali leaders who were also loyal to the British rulers. They were persuaded to join the Muslim League and struggle for a separate Muslim country. This was considered to be a turning point for Bengali leadership, as the majority of Muslims in Bengal were struggling against British rule alongside congress. As observed by Ahmed (2004), with this, the historical Bengali union for centuries for Banga-Mata (Mother Bengal) came to an end. The call of Muslim nationhood and the belief that they would be in the leading position in the proposed new country lured them into cooperation with the Muslim League. But as soon as Pakistan came to existence, Bengali leaders realized that Pakistan would not be a country for any nation but a country for a Muslim army. The civil and military establishment took charge of the country and began to exercise their oppressive measures against democratic forces.

Although in the beginning the Bengali leadership was committed to the concept of the two-nation theory and tried for some accommodation with the ruling alliance, it seems they were not aware of the intention of the military establishment. As a goodwill gesture, Bengali leaders even surrendered some of their seats in the constituent assembly to accommodate Muhajir leaders—such as Liaquat Ali Khan, Sardar Nishtar, and Maulana Shabbir Ahmed Usmani—but their goodwill did not help them in the corridors of power (Ahmed 2004).

The game for control between East and West Pakistan began even before Pakistan emerged on the map of the world. Viceroy Lord Mountbatten mentioned in his July 11, 1947, report that "Muslim League High Command themselves take a good deal less interest in East Pakistan than Western Pakistan and I am afraid East Bengal is at the bottom of the priority list." The gap between East and West Pakistan had widened during the government of Governor-General Ghulam Muhammad, Iskander Mirza, Ayub Khan, and Yahya Khan (Ahmed 2004). The resistance against the perceived injustices to Bengalis was led by H. S. Suhrawardy and Fazal ul Haque, while some of the Bengali leaders—like Nazimuddin, Mohammad Ali Bogra, and Nurul Amin—became collaborators, and their services were used by the army in the scheme of countering Bengali national sentiments in the name of Islamic brotherhood.

With the realization that the military establishment and its allies were determined to run the country from the top with a colonial mentality, Suhrawardy tried to change the political structure of Pakistan by forming a new political party—the Awami Muslim League. It posed a great challenge for the old Muslim League. When Suhrawardy became the prime minister, he enjoyed widespread support both from east and west of the country. This was considered to be the beginning of a new path or a new way to put Pakistan on the road of a democratic system that could have led both wings into harmony (Choudhury 1972).

In a democratic system of government, usually the majority group of people would lead state legislation and the executive and would not fear losing their culture, language, and economic status. Although Pakistan has started its political journey with a parliamentary system aiming to have a federal constitution, both the parliamentary system and the federal constitutional mottoes were not genuine. The constitution was framed to provide masks for the ruling alliance (Choudhury 1972). Bengalis, who formed the majority of the population in Pakistan, not only were kept out of power but their language, culture, and heritage also became vulnerable. Urdu, the language of a few thousand immigrants from North India, was declared as the national language of the state. It caused strong opposition from Bengalis (Islam 1978). Several people were killed in Dhaka and other cities in East Pakistan during the language riots of the early 1950s. It was the beginning of distrust among Bengalis and the rise of their national sentiments.

When Ayub Khan took over in 1958, it widened the gap even further between East and West Pakistan. Sheikh Mujibur Rahman, who became the leader of the Awami League after the murder of Suhrawardy, was implicated in a treason case by the military authorities. This made him a hero among the Bengali youth. He was popularly named as Bangabandhu (friend of Bengal). The popular uprising under the banner of the Awami League and National Awami Party in 1969 forced Ayub Khan to resign, and then came the martial law of Yahya who suspended the constitution until the 1970 elections. The Awami League with Shiekh Mujibur Rahman's Six-Point Agenda swept the poll in East Pakistan and won 160 out of a total of three hundred national assembly seats in the general elections held in 1970. Mujibur Rahman was refused from forming the new civilian government by the ruling alliance. The refusal of power to the majority party of the 1970 general elections was a clear message to East Pakistan that their government was not acceptable. Seeing no role for them in Pakistan, the demand for an independent Bengal came into being (Choudhury 1972).

To counter the Bengali demands for the convening of the national assembly, a crackdown was initiated against the Awami League and its leader, Sheikh Mujibur Rahman, was arrested on March 25, 1971. As agitation erupted against the political crackdown, the army began a ruthless military operation, and thousands of Bengalis were killed during nine months of confrontation between the army and the Bengali youth organized under the banner of Mukti Bahini (the liberation army). The army massacred politicians, students, teachers, and intellectuals and raped thousands of women. The plan was to kill as many Bengalis as possible. It was considered to be a calculated and systematic genocide plan to bring Bengalis on their knees so that they would never dare to stand against the rule of the military from West Pakistan (Rummel 1990). At a conference on February 22, 1971, the military president of Pakistan general Yahya Khan's statement is recorded saying, "Kill three million of them (Bengalis) and the rest will eat out of our hands." On March 26, 1971, the Pakistani army launched its Operation Searchlight in east wing (now Bangladesh) to quell the uprising, and it was soon cleared that the general did mean to kill millions when he said it. During the nine months of brutal army action, three million people—including, students, teachers, intellectuals, women, and children—were killed and up to thirty million were made homeless (Alston 2015). While millions of people were fleeing to India and the numbers of refugees were rapidly rising at the Indian border, ironically, the major powers of the world were unable to move (Sission and Rose 1990). The disastrous humanitarian crisis of the Bengalis forced the Indian government to intervene, as there was no hope left in New Delhi for any peaceful solution to the conflict. The only option taken by Pakistani rulers was the use of ruthless military prowess to deal with the popular uprising in the majority province of their country (Siddiq 1978).

While discussing the causes of the secession of Bengalis from Pakistan, it is interesting to observe that the whole federal and constitutional claim of Pakistan was a fraud. From the very beginning, the alliance of the military, mullahs, and Muhajirs had been ruling the Allah-given country in a colonial manner. Exclusion from political corridors of power was the basic element of the anger of the Bengalis. Despite being the majority of the country, Bengalis were excluded from central government. Except for a short period of thirteen months during 1956–57, H. S. Suhrawardy became the prime minister of Pakistan. But he was forced to resign and banned from politics by General Ayub Khan. Earlier, Khawaja Nazimuddin suffered the same fate. The ruling alliance not only ran the central government but also took key posts of the provincial administration of East Pakistan. The army stationed in East Pakistan was to watch over the administration to exclude any chance of genuine representatives of Bengali in the power corridors (Choudhury 1972). The language issue was the triggering element in the alienation of Bengalis. After gaining full control of the state, Punjabis and their allies in the ruling alliance began ruthless economic exploitation. Bengalis believed that only their jute production earned more than 50 percent of state revenue while the budgetary allocation for East Pakistan was only a fraction of revenue generated from their land. The refusal to accept Bengali language, culture, and basic democratic rights exacerbated the fragile relationship between Bengalis and the state of Pakistan. The Muhajir intellectuals and writers began to portray a historical and cultural history of the region that negated the existence of thousand-year old Bengali culture and traditions. The imposition of Urdu as national language and desecration and mutilation of sociocultural traditions were major factors that gave impetus for the demand for separation from the state.

The birth of Bengal was painful and bloody. It was the irony of Pakistani politics that the very people who played the biggest role to create Pakistan had to fight yet another catastrophic war with the state they cherished and joined in the name of Muslim brotherhood. The way Pakistan was carved out of India, it is not surprising that after twenty-four years, it went into another catastrophic secession between its two wings, east and west, consuming three million Bengali lives. After losing its east wing, there was a general belief that Pakistani rulers had learned a lesson and would allow the country to include its other nations and political institutions in running the country; but unfortunately, the attitude of the Pakistani establishment was unchanged toward Sindhi, Baloch, and Pashtun nations. It's been forty-eight years since Bengalis decided to secede from the religious state, but it appears that Pakistan's problem was and still is that the ruling alliance has been refusing to accept a constitutional and democratic system where representatives of all people are included in the decision-making for the country. The military establishment is still refusing to admit that Pakistan is a multinational state.

During the colonial era, powerful countries drew some unjust and troubling border lines around the globe, dividing people and their homeland for their interest and ignoring the history, culture, and heritage of people. Since the departure of colonial powers, these unnatural lines have been triggering conflicts in many parts of the world. The general feeling is that decolonization was completed during the 1960s; it seems we forget that our modern world is still embroiled in various political disputes and conflicts that are the consequences of the colonial era. When the British divided India in 1947, they created Pakistan as a client state, and they were not concerned whether it would become a democratic state or not. Years later, Western powers realized that creating Pakistan was a good decision for their Cold War strategies in the region, as the largest democracy of India was not playing their games and they were suspicious about India—especially the Nixon government considered India as part of the Soviet Bloc. The United Kingdom and the United States used Pakistan during the Cold War, and in exchange, Pakistan received military aid from them and built a strong army. They were not interested in how Pakistan ran its local businesses or treated its population as long as its foreign policies were aligned with their interests. It is widely believed that Western powers, including the Nixon administration in the USA, were fully aware of General Yahya's monstrous plans for East Pakistan, but they had decided to remain silent while he went on slaughtering Bengalis in 1971 (Bass 2013).

In spite of having the United Nations Charter on the right of self-determination, the UN Convention on the Prevention and Punishment of the Crime of Genocide, and the Western world's close focus on South Asia, General Yahya was not only able to bar an elected party from forming government in Pakistan but was also given a free hand and space to murder as many Bengalis as he wanted, which became one of the darkest periods of the modern world. After the Second World War and the Holocaust, words like "never again, never again" began to resound throughout the international community. The immediate preventive measures against genocide and crimes against humanity brought great hope for a new emerging world, but unfortunately, since the adoption of the Convention on Genocide and Crimes against Humanity by the United Nations in 1948, we have seen a repetition of heinous crime against humanity in many parts of the world. Apart from the legal phraseology of words *genocide* and *crimes against humanity* and some international rules and principle against these terms, the world did not do enough to prevent such evil crimes against humanity. In other words, the world has failed to protect people from genocide, crimes against humanity, and ethnic cleansing; thus, populace of Bangladesh, Rwanda, Cambodia, East Timor, South Sudan, Syria, and many others had to face mass killings in the modern global village, and only a handful of perpetrators have been convicted by the International Criminal Court. The world will not succeed in preventing evil crimes such as genocide until it changes its course of action in dealing with unfolding conflicts around the globe. To avoid such gruesome crimes against humanity, the United Nations should take tangible, rigorous, and timely actions.

Since the end of World War II, the world has been asserting a desire to improve the life of human beings regardless of their race, religion, and geography, and people also began to demand their democratic rights. They want their rights to be protected from harm and to be recognized as equal members of their society. They desire to handle their own social, cultural, economic, and political matters. But it is understood that as the people push for their legitimate rights, they are met with ruthless and oppressive measures in many parts of the world. Therefore, the United Nations should take human rights issues seriously and reach out to those who are at immediate risk of being slaughtered, such as the NATO intervention in Libya in 2011. They should not wait to count millions of dead people.

C H A P T E R

EIGHT

THE BALOCH RIGHT OF SELF-DETERMINATION

The Baloch conflict with Pakistan and Iran is one of the unresolved issues of the postcolonial world. Balochistan was occupied by the British in 1839 and later divided into many parts. After the British withdrawal from India, the Baloch state of Kalat declared its independence on June 11, 1947. However, the newly created religious state of Pakistan, with the help and agreement of the former colonial power, managed to annex it. Since then, the Baloch and Pakistan are engaged in a long-drawn-out bloody conflict.

The Baloch and Balochistan

It is difficult to find the early traces of the Baloch people in recorded history. During their hard historical journey, the Baloch tribes have seen various persecutions and massacres. It is believed that the most devastating genocide of the Baloch people occurred during the Sassanid Empire (531–579 AD). According to the Persian historical account *Shahnameh*, the Baloch were assumed to be completely wiped out during the reign of King Khosrow, as he saw them as a group of wild, unruly people and condemned them to death. Despite the powerful king's genocidal wishes, somehow some of the Baloch tribes survived in deep mountains and regrouped against the odds (Dashti 2012).

The racial origin of the Baloch has been discussed by many, and it has been established that they are among the Indo-Iranic tribes of Aryan origin who migrated from Central Asia many thousands of years ago. This has been established taking into account the historical events in the region and their language, culture, physical, and mental characteristics. As observed by prominent Baloch scholar Jan Dashti, the Balochi language is one of the Indo-European languages of the Central Asian group like Kurdish and Persian. The linguistic roots of these groups of languages indicate that they must have had close interactions in the past (Dashti 1982). Baloch historian Dr. Naseer Dashti came up with the theory that the Baloch originate from Balashagan. He believes that the Baloch and some other Indo-Iranic tribes migrated from Central Asia toward the Caspian Sea and the eastern highland of Iran around 2000 BC. The Baloch settled in the western Caspian region that was called Balashakan or Balashagan, and the inhabitants of that region were known as Balashchik. These tribes of Balashakan were compelled to migrate. After many hundreds of years of the migratory process, they settled in the region that is now called Balochistan; and from Balaschik, they became the Baloch of the modern era (Dashti 2012).

Balochistan remained part of various ancient powers in the region, such as Persians, Greek, Mauryan, and Sassanids. The invasion of Arabs brought some of the far-reaching changes in the whole region, including in the life of Baloch people. The Arabs arrived in the seventh century AD with new social, economic, cultural, and belief systems. Zoroastrian religion was replaced with Islam, and there was a considerable shift in the social and political perspectives of people. Iranian God Ahura Mazda was replaced with Arabian God Allah (Dashti 2012). The new religion of Islam became part of people's everyday life, and the powerful Arab reign spanned around 150 years. However, amid all these historical happenings around and in their homeland, the Baloch persisted as a single unit and preserved their social and cultural ethos and their Balochi language (Marri 2007).

The decaying Arab rule was replaced by regional dynasties of Saffarids, Buyids, and Samanids during 819–1003. These dynastic powers were no less cruel to the local people. They also massacred the Baloch population on various occasions, which pushed them further to Makran and Turan. On the other hand, this period is considered to be one of the most important points for the Baloch tribes in terms of their character and unity for the following centuries. The Balochi language, culture, and national sentiment among Baloch tribes began to shape a unified force as a Baloch people. Therefore, the landmass under their control came to be known as Balochistan, meaning the country of the Baloch people. They were called Baloch and spoke Balochi language; therefore, the land they inhabited became Balochistan. They survived and gradually established a nation-state called Khanate of Kalat, which lasted about three hundred years (Dashti 2012).

Balochistan is the vast landmass extending from southeastern Iran to Helmand, Farah, and Kandahar in Afghanistan, the east bank of the Sindh River and the Indian Ocean. In the south, the Indian Ocean separates Balochistan from the Arabian Peninsula. Present-day Balochistan is divided among Iran, Pakistan, and Afghanistan.

Archaeological evidence suggests that Balochistan has been an important route between the civilization of Indus valley and Mesopotamia. Balochistan was divided into numerous provinces during the Achaemenes Empire, such as Maka and Zaranka, which later became known as Makran and Sistan. Alexander the Great marched through Balochistan during his campaign to conquer the world in 330 BC. The Greeks called the southern part of Balochistan Gedrosia, and during the Arab reign, the area encompassing Sarwan and Jhalawan was called Turan (Dashti 2012).

When Baloch tribes consolidated and strengthened their power over the vast area of Balochistan, the first Baloch state emerged under Khanate of Kalat in the mid-seventeenth century. This confederacy of Baloch tribes began to rule over all regions of Balochistan. It is believed that during the reign of Mir Naseer Khan I, Balochistan extended up to Hasanabad (Sistan) Helmand River as far as Rudbar, Nimroz, and Farah in Afghanistan. In western areas, it extended from Makran and Sarhad up to Kerman in present-day Iran. In the east, the rule of Khanate of Kalat reached up to Dera Ismail Khan and

Dera Ghazi Khan regions of present-day Pakistan. In southern areas, Balochistan bordered on Sindh, and the Persian Gulf separated it from Oman and other modern-day Gulf States (Dashti 2012).

The Khanate of Kalat

During medieval times, various tribal alliances emerged in different parts of Balochistan. The tribal confederacy became a common need for the survival and the protection of their collective land and possessions. The structure of this unity was shaped to deal with internal and external matters based on local and central authority methods. Many Baloch tribes formed unions in different parts of Balochistan, but then their unions did not last long, and the conflict erupted over authority, pastures, land, and possessions. For example, Rind and Laashaar's alliance was a strong union alongside many others in the beginning, but later they went into a full war against each other with far-reaching consequences. The Rind and Laashaar conflict destabilized the spirit of a Baloch nation-state. On the other hand, they began to take a side in the Indian conflict between Suri and Mughal rulers, which had weakened their positions even further in Balochistan (Dashti 2012).

During the sixteenth century, Balochistan was divided between Mughal and Safavid empires. The Safavid dynasty began to decline in the early seventeenth century, and it faced numerous uprisings in Iran. The powerful dynasty was losing control in many parts of its territory, and the death of King Shah Abbas I exacerbated the situation even further. His successor, Shah Safi, was unable to consolidate his position and bring the decaying dynasty together. Various groups and provinces under the supremacy of the Safavid king took advantage of the weakening rulers and pushed for more authority over their respective areas. On the other side of the Baloch horizon, the Mughal Empire was on a path to destruction in India. The arrival of European colonial powers on the Indian shores in the guise of trade and business was a sign of the falling Mughal Empire and the beginning of European influence in the entire region. With the weakening of these powerful empires, one confederacy of the Baloch tribes in 1666 under the chieftaincy of Mir Ahmed established the Khanate of Kalat in

Turan, which later extended its control over the whole Baloch region. This was the beginning of a Baloch nation-state (Dashti 2012).

It seems that the seventeenth century became a significant stage for the Baloch people. The dispersed Baloch tribes in the huge Baloch landmass succeeded in their long struggle for a nation-state. The establishment of the Kalat state was a collective and larger unity among Baloch tribes as a political force to run their state affairs under the leadership of Khan. In the history of all nations, there have been specific times when they evolved from one stage into another. It was that time and century for the Baloch tribes to enter the next phase of nationhood. As observed by Dashti (2012), the emergence of the Khanate of Kalat shaped the destiny of the Baloch nation for three hundred years.

The Arrival of the British

The Portuguese voyage of Vasco da Gama to India in the fifteenth century was the opening arrival from Europe. He was the first to discover the passage round the Cape of Good Hope to Hindustan (Mill 1817). Thereafter, the quest of India was followed by Dutch, French, and Great Britain. The Portuguese had explored Hindustan without any rival for a whole century. The rule of the Portuguese Empire was gradually extended to as far as the coast of Makran in Balochistan during the seventeeth century (Narayanan 2006). The British arrived as traders of the East India Company. However, after a few decades, they not only forced their European competitors out of India but also began to rule the vast landmass after the collapse of the Mughal Empire. When the British forces overpowered their last rival—the French—in 1799, they became the sole ruler of the Indian subcontinent until 1947 (Naravane 2007).

The Indian subcontinent became the focal point for Great Britain for its colonial ambition, and it was concerned about the advancing influence of the czar's Russia in the region. After losing the Americas, the British Empire asserted its control in Africa and also in the Indian subcontinent by introducing various methods to secure its possessions from any internal and external threat. They decided to expand their area of control further into Balochistan, Iran, and Afghanistan to prevent Russia from closing in and threatening the interests of the empire. To proceed further into Iran and Afghanistan, it was inevitable to triumph over Balochistan before advancing toward Iran and Afghanistan's borders (Dashti 2012).

The British Occupation of Balochistan

While the Great Game of Russia and Great Britain was gaining momentum for more areas of influence in the Middle East, India, and Central Asia, the Baloch land became the most important as a gateway leading to Iran-Afghanistan and beyond to Central Asia. The military power of Khanate of Kalat was no match for such a great empire as Britain. However, Khan Mir Mehrab Khan II resisted bravely until he met his death. The capital of Balochistan, Kalat, fell to the British on November 13, 1839, which brought to an end of three hundred years of the Baloch state.

The British incursion into Kalat and the killing of the head of the Baloch state was a heavy blow to the political structure of Balochistan. The Baloch resisted the occupation, and the resistance movement against the British occupation began in different parts of Balochistan soon after the occupation of Kalat. The legitimate heir to the throne, Mir Naseer Khan II, rallied the Baloch tribes. However, after some years, a peace process began in January 1841 with the British. Mir Naseer Khan II was recognized as the khan of Kalat by the British, and the khan accepted the British supremacy over Balochistan (Naseer Dashti 2012).

The British imposed various treaties on the khan, including free movement and the stationing of British armed forces all over Balochistan. The construction of the railway tracks and the expansion of the Indo-European Telegraph Line through the territory of Kalat and also the division of Balochistan into four parts were major events. In the 1876 treaty between the khan and the British, the British expected the khan's full support in terms of protecting the interests of the British Empire in his country. In return, the British recognized the internal autonomy of Balochistan.

The British were aiming to sustain their positions in Balochistan and also save Iran and Afghanistan from Russian influence. The appeasement policy toward Iran and Afghanistan resulted in the division of Balochistan and the incorporation of some parts into Iran and Afghanistan. The division of Balochistan was brought about under Perso-Baloch Boundary Commission, McMahon Commission, and Durand Commission (Baloch 1987).

During the nineteenth century, leaders of the Baloch tribes in western Balochistan and Iran reached an agreement that recognized Sardar Hussain Khan as the ruler of Balochistan; but in return, he accepted the supremacy of Persia over western Balochistan. After the death of Sardar Hussain Khan in 1907, Mir Bahram Khan became the chief of the Baloch, and he pushed for more control over western Balochistan. His efforts and determination succeeded, and he signed a treaty with the British in 1916. It was the recognition of his authority over the southern areas of Balochistan where the British had real concern about the security of their expeditionary and the telegraph line.

The Qajar era of Persia is considered to be one of the darkest times of the Baloch people. They were subjected to massacre, displacement, and slavery. However, when the Qajar dynasty began to decline during the nineteenth century, thee Baloch regained their positions under the leadership of the Barakzai clan. When Mir Dost Muhammad became the head of Baloch chiefdom in 1921, he not only consolidated his position over western Balochistan but also brought forward administrative reforms and unified all tribal leaders under his chiefdom. He established a good relationship with Kalat and also extended his diplomatic relationships to the neighboring countries, like Afghanistan and Oman (Dashti 2017).

The Turkic origin Qajar dynasty ruled over Persia from 1789 to 1925. In the early nineteenth century, two great powers, Great Britain and Russia, extended their interests into Qajar's Persia. The dynasty began to tumble under the pressure of these big powers and lost its control over various parts of Persia. The British changed their position and began to groom a new dynasty in the region, which later became known as the Pahlavi dynasty. The Qajar was replaced by the Pahlavi dynasty in 1925, and Persia became Iran. As Reza Khan emerged as Shah of Iran, he began to assert his authority over those areas where Iran had lost control during its political turmoil. When Reza Shah sustained his position in some parts of Iran, he sent threatening messages to Mir Dost Muhammad demanding to submit to his rule or face the consequences. The Baloch leadership rejected his demand and began to rally Baloch forces against the looming war with Iran. The war between Baloch and Iran began in 1928 and lasted around one year. The phenomenal resistance of the Baloch forces in the face of the well-armed army with sophisticated artillery was even noticed and acknowledged by the commanding general of the Iranian army. Thousands of Baloch were killed and displaced during the one-year war. Areas of western Balochistan fell one by one to the advancing Iranian army. The head of western Balochistan, Mir Dost Muhammad, was captured and later hanged in Tehran by the Shah regime in 1931. However, the Baloch resistance continued in different parts of western Balochistan against Iran and the British authorities from 1920 to 1938 (Dashti 2017). As the Baloch resistance weakened, the Pahlavi regime eventually incorporated western Balochistan into Iran with the help of Great Britain, bringing an end to western Balochistan after years of wars and bloodshed.

The Second World War from 1938 to 1945 brought drastic changes in the entire world. The power of the British Empire had shrunk during the First World War, and the Second World War brought the vast empire to its knees. One of the most powerful colonizers of the world had no choice but to leave its possessions and the colonies around the globe. Where the departure of Great Britain from Asia and Africa paved the way for many nations to regain their freedoms there, it left behind unnatural demarcations, disputes, and divisions in those parts of the world. In the case of the Indian subcontinent, it created a pseudostate of Pakistan in the name of religion that resulted in far-reaching consequences for Balochistan (Dashti 2017).

Under the occupation of Iran and Pakistan, the people of Balochistan has been denied the basic human rights in Iran and Pakistan. Many Baloch cities and towns have been completely changed over the last seven decades, and the Baloch is becoming a minority group of people in their homeland. The social, economic, and cultural activities of Baloch have been limited and watched by state agencies. Both parts of Balochistan have been changed into military garrisons that keep terrorizing the Baloch population. Despite the draconian policy of Iran and Pakistan for more than seven decades, the spirit of Baloch as a nation seems stronger than ever before.

Fall of the British Empire and Balochistan

After two great wars in the twentieth century, far-reaching changes occurred in many parts of the world. Numerous big powers crumbled resulting in the emergence of various new states on the map of the world. The First World War weakened the British Empire, and the Second World War destroyed the British administrative and economic structure in Europe, Asia, and Africa, bringing down the vast empire. The demand for liberation and decolonization began to echo from Asia to Africa in the crumbling empire. As the struggle for independence intensified in the British colonies, it became clear that British forces could not sustain their positions in the extended colonies around the globe (Low 1993).

The national struggle of India was one of the largest political movements relying on people power. The civil resistance led by Mahatma Gandhi was a mass nonviolent political mobilization of Indian people against colonial forces. The unique methods of nonviolence and noncooperation of Mahatma Gandhi became the source of unity among Indians, which brought the mighty British authority to its knees in India (Carter 2009). The peaceful and noncooperation resistance under the leadership of Mahatma Gandhi gained momentum during 1920–1930, and it was obvious that British forces could not save their possessions in India for much longer. The desperate Cripps Mission headed by Sir Stafford Cripps to India in 1942 failed, as the Congress rejected the offer of self-rule by the end of the Second World War. The Quit India movement intensified while the British tried to sustain their position in India. Addison (1975) observed that once the British realized that the exit from India was inevitable, they sought different ways to remain influential in the subcontinent. The idea of dividing India into the religious lines of Hindu and Muslim came into play. This was not the first time that the British Empire used religion to divide historically harmonized people. The empire used various methods to divide and rule, and religion was one of the most useful instruments for that purpose. The divisive methods began as soon as the British set foot on Indian soil, marking lines between areas and people on various grounds. The use of tribe, ethnic group, and religions severed the empire's purposes well around the world. In India, religion became the decisive force for the British Empire against the people who lived together for a thousand years without any religious dispute. Carving out Pakistan from India in the name of religion was the most disastrous event for the whole region and the generations to follow. It was all done to keep division, destabilize the subcontinent, and remain influential in the form of Pakistan.

The British authorities in India ushered some Muslim leaders under the umbrella of the Muslim League to justify that Muslims do not want to live with Hindus in one country so they could divide India in the guise of the professed two-nation theory. The creation of Pakistan and the Hindu-Muslim division were the most important achievements of the British Empire in India, which reached its catastrophic end in 1947. Jinnah and the Muslim League used Islam as an ideology of the Muslim nation, which resulted in the confused form of Pakistan on August 14, 1947, which included East Pakistan, the present-day Bangladesh. The creation of Pakistan ultimately resulted in the demise of the three-hundred-year-old Baloch state (Dashti 2012). After eight months of freedom from British rule, Balochistan was also forcibly included in the Muslim country of Pakistan. This was one of the rare cases in history of colonial powers that have changed the identity of people in this way (Bates 2011).

Annexation of Balochistan into Pakistan

In a Cold War context, the newborn Muslim states of Pakistan, India, and the Persian Gulf were vulnerable to Soviet advances; therefore, efforts were made to save the region from the influence of the Soviet Union. The British were leaving the Indian subcontinent as a colonial power but wanted to remain influential in some other ways in the region. At the time of British withdrawal from India, some leased areas of Balochistan and some parts of Afghanistan were a province of British India in the name of British Balochistan. The British administration handed over British Balochistan to Pakistan on August 14, 1947, as a gesture of goodwill, violating the lease treaty with the Khanate of Kalat. Nine months after the British departure from India, Pakistan also invaded the Khanate of Kalat, bringing to an end the Baloch state (Dashti 2017).

The Eastern Balochistan areas of Quetta, Marri-Bugti Agency, Sibi, and Chagai were called the British Balochistan after they were leased out to the British Empire in 1880. British Balochistan was under the direct control of the British authority in India, while the sovereignty of the Khanate of Kalat was recognized through various treaties from 1854 to 1878. Handing over the British Balochistan to the newborn state of Pakistan was a clear violation of international law. According to international obligations, the British authorities were bound to return the Baloch lands to the khan of Kalat. A group of attorneys was appointed by the khan to launch a case against the decision of the British authority. Mohammed Ali Jinnah was chosen by the khan to represent the case of Balochistan, which was a great mistake in every aspect of regional politics by the khan. Mr. Jinnah was on the path of becoming the leader of the newborn country of Pakistan, which would lead to the demise of the whole Balochistan.

Balochistan was declared an independent country on August 12, 1947, two days before Pakistan was created. As soon as Balochistan became independent, the khan asserted his aims and ambitions to build a prosperous state according to Baloch values, code, and traditions. He affirmed that the Baloch country would establish a good and equal relationship with its neighboring states. The elections were held in Balochistan, and peace and tranquility were assured to the Baloch people. As the Baloch state proceeded to establish its authorities and institutions after the British colonial era, the new Islamic state of Pakistan began to intimidate and manipulate the khan under the pretext of Muslim brotherhood. It was obvious from the creation of Pakistan that it would carry the peculiar image of a Muslim nation and would sell this notion within and into the entire region. However, the theory of Muslim brotherhood at the expense of losing a country, identity, and the thousand years of Baloch history did not go down well among the Baloch people, arguably because the roots of the Baloch nation were deeply imbedded in Baloch history and the land they lived in for thousands of years. It was also clear that the relationship of Baloch people with their homeland and history was much stronger than their religious belief system (Heeg 2011).

The parliament of Balochistan rejected the Pakistani suggestion of joining the Islamic State (Ray 1998).The new Muslim state of Pakistan used various tactics and intimidation to convince Baloch leaders for the merger with Pakistan, but they refused every attempt from the Pakistani side. After complete rejection from the khan and both Houses of Parliament, the Pakistan Army marched on Kalat on March 27, 1948, and forced the khan to sign the merger agreement.

Khan's younger brother, Prince Abdul Karim, with the silent approval of the khan, declared a revolt demanding the withdrawal of the Pakistan Army from Kalat. He published a manifesto on behalf of his Baloch National Liberation Committee rejecting the forced accession agreement and demanded the complete withdrawal of the Pakistan Army from Balochistan (Harrison 1981). After a short-lived guerrilla warfare from bordering Afghanistan, the prince and his comrades agreed to put their guns down in exchange for amnesty. The government of Pakistan broke the amnesty pact and arrested and imprisoned the prince on his return to Kalat. This was the first of numerous broken promises between Pakistan and Baloch people. This event would lead to waves of armed conflicts between Baloch and the state of Pakistan. The recent insurgency in Balochistan is a continuum of struggles that started in 1948 after the invasion of Pakistan. The present armed conflict in Balochistan is quite different from the ones in 1948, 1958, 1962, and 1973 in its scale and international attention and recognition, but the demands and the goal are the same: the right to self-determination of the Baloch people (Heeg 2011).

The Essence of the Baloch Demand for the Right of Self-Determination

Many nations have succeeded in regaining their country and independence after the colonial era, and there are various ethnic groups and nations who are still seeking to navigate their way to dignity and freedom. The unjust and unnatural mapmaking of colonial powers during the nineteenth and twentieth centuries had completely ignored the plight of those people. The homelands of many nations were marked and divided into different countries, and they were confined between unnatural boundary lines. The British authorities were most famous in their ambition for drawing lines and dividing people during their imperial rule. In the case of Balochistan, the British did not only divide it but they also gifted away the historical Baloch land to Iran, Afghanistan, and their client state of Pakistan. Since the British departure from the Indian subcontinent, there have been five episodes of insurgency in Balochistan. The first resistance began as soon as Pakistan invaded Balochistan in 1948 (Heeg 2011).

According to Baloch scholar Jan Dashti, Pakistan was created under a peculiar notion of a Muslim nation in the history of nations. The highest-ranking bureaucrats and political leaders were imported from northern India who had no cultural or historical roots in their new home. It was also strange that the language of a few thousand Indian emigrants was declared the official language of the Muslim state of Pakistan. The religious ideology of Pakistan and its identity were alien to the local people who were becoming part of a country that was oddly claiming to be a Muslim nation-state. He observed that as soon as Pakistan was carved out of India, it landed right under the boots of the army. The God-given country was given a centralized framework under the wing of the army, which would lead the Muslim country to its disintegration in 1971 (Dashti 1987).

Since its creation, Pakistan has faced the challenge of a separate identity that meant completely different from India in all aspects. Breaking away from an ancient civilization with only a thin claim of Muslim identity, Pakistan had to struggle to construct its own culture, language, and history. Therefore, as soon as Pakistan was separated from India, it began to distort the history of the region to draw an image of a new Muslim nation. Instead of recognizing and harmonizing the local national history and traditions, Pakistan began to borrow history and heroes from alien sources. As the country was created in the name of Islam, it ended up borrowing from the various characters of Muslim invaders who ruled and plundered the region before the British arrival in the Indian subcontinent. In this long search for identity, Pakistan not only failed to solve the problems of its alleged Muslim nation but it also generated new issues and confusion for the local people. It seems that Pakistan is stuck among the army, the mullah, and the fake identity as a Muslim nation and unable to become a modern state (Jaffrelot 2002). Pakistan is still carrying the so-called two-nation theory of Hindu and Muslim that should have been buried within the creation of Pakistan. The image of a Muslim nation cannot keep these nations together until they are recognized as nations and treated equally under a just federal governing system (Marri 2007).

The history of a nation is based on territory, language, culture, and a collective ethnic social contract in which all members identify themselves with it. A nation has an enduring social and political history—a relative moral, mental, and cultural unity of its inhabitants who consciously adhere to the state and its rules. Pakistan lacked that characteristic of a nation precisely because of existing different nations before Pakistan was even born. They have their deep-rooted history, language, culture, territories, and social milieu. Pakistan has not only failed to recognize these realities but also has been practicing colonial methods to offset those failures. The strategy to use Islam to manipulate the Baloch and other ethnic groups of Pakistan for integration into a Muslim-nation concept and the creation of radical Islamists against its neighboring countries have been causing far-reaching changes in the social and cultural behavior of brotherly nations of Pakistan. The Pakistani-sponsored jihadists are not only intensifying the regional conflict with India, Afghanistan, and Iran but also exporting radical Islamic ideology around the world (Jaffrelot 2002).

Various factors are contributing to the persistent Baloch struggle for the right of self-determination since Balochistan was incorporated into Pakistan in 1948. Firstly, Balochistan was a separate country with a separate nation with its history, tradition, values, and culture. It was neither part of British India nor part of the partition of India in 1947. British had recognized Balochistan as a country and signed numerous treaties with the khan, the head of the Baloch state. Secondly, the Baloch state was divided by the British imperial administration into different parts. Some of the areas were gifted away by the British to Iran and Afghanistan, and the rest was abandoned at the mercy of Iran and Pakistan on their messy departure from the region. Thirdly, Baloch was betrayed by the leader of the newly emerging Islamic state of Pakistan, Mohammed Ali Jinnah. Mr. Jinnah was hired by the naive khan of Kalat as his lawyer to defend and represent the case of his country, but when he became the first governor-general of Pakistan in 1947, he authorized the annexation of Balochistan into Pakistan despite recognizing Balochistan as a sovereign state. Furthermore, Pakistan has never recognized the legitimate rights of Baloch people over their natural resources since its occupation (Dashti 2017).

The division of Balochistan into three countries by the British rulers was followed by ill-treatment in their new host countries. Exclusion from mainstream polity and the continued refusal of democratic rights in these totalitarian states and the oppressive measures against them fed the Baloch national resistance movement since the departure of the British Empire. The Baloch had never accepted the thought of losing their identity as a nation for some bizarre notion of a Muslim nation under the boots of one national army. The invasion of Pakistan in 1948 was illegal in every aspect of international legal norms. The Baloch not only denounced the wrongful act of Pakistan but also revolted against it without having the means and support. The Baloch leadership instantly realized that the British already had given the green light to their client state against Balochistan and they would not gain any tangible leverage against Pakistan's occupation except recording their protest against the illegal invasion of Pakistan.

After the brief rebellion against Pakistani incursion, the Baloch began a political mobilization to continue their struggle for recognition of their national rights and autonomous status. They launched a new party called Ustaman Gal (UG) in 1955 aiming to gain support and joined hands with other emerging political forces in Pakistan. The newborn Muslim state of Pakistan was mainly focused on sustaining its control over the area through its military power and suppressing the voice of masses for a modern, just, and democratic state. The National Awami Party was established in 1957; the political program and the demands of NAP also attracted the attention of Baloch leadership, and they joined the party. But the Pakistani army had no space for a civilian system in the country, and it was not a surprise when the army declared martial law and took direct control of Pakistan on October 27, 1958.

Initially, the Baloch did not give up hope for the restoration of the Khanate of Kalat even within the framework of Pakistan. Various Baloch tribal leaders rallied behind Mir Ahmad Yar Khan. The negotiations between Baloch and Pakistani president Iskander Mirza failed. The demand for the restoration of Khanate of Khan was rejected, which was followed by more army crackdowns on political activities in Balochistan. The army raided the Palace of Khan, killed and wounded many Baloch, and arrested the khan. He was incarcerated on the charges of conspiring against the state of Pakistan. Besides the khan's arrest, thousands of Baloch political activists, including Prince Abdul Karim, were put behind bars by the military administration of General Ayub Khan, which had triggered a decade of unrest in Balochistan (Dashti 2017).

Despite the heavy-handed military actions in Balochistan, that phase of resistance continued for many years. Alongside various groups of tribal leaders, Nawab Nauroz Khan joined the guerrilla war against Pakistan, and his group fought until 1959. Nawab Nauroz Khan was one of the leading figures of the rebellion. His fighters carried out guerrilla attacks, and it was difficult for the Pakistan Army to completely defeat him while he was attacking from the deep mountain region. Therefore, the army began negotiations with Nawab to cease his guerrilla warfare; and in exchange, he was guaranteed by taking the oath on the Koran (the holy Muslim book) that his group would not face any kind of charges or persecution. After the deal, Nawab Nauroz Khan and his companions laid down their guns in May 1959. The aged Nawab, his sons, and their followers were arrested immediately after they were disarmed. They were put on a nominal trial and convicted of treason in a military court. Nawab Nauroz received a life imprisonment sentence, and later he died in Kohlu jail. It is believed that he was around ninety years old when he met his death in captivity. His six family members were subsequently hanged, and some of his followers were given long imprisonment sentences.

After the arrest and execution of Nawab Nauroz's family members, the tension continued between the Baloch and the ruling army of Pakistan. The Baloch resistance gained momentum when Mengal, Mari, and Bugti tribes joined the armed struggle. The new wave of the uprising was more organized and covered various parts of Balochistan. The fighting intensified and continued between Baloch guerilla and Pakistani armed forces for several years. During that period of the war, the Pakistani army used its heavy artillery indiscriminately against the Baloch freedom fighters and the population, destroying Baloch villages and killing thousands of civilians. The armed conflict of that phase extended from 1958 to 1971. On the political scene, despite arrest and intimidation, the Baloch leadership gathered under the umbrella of NAP, which was a strong growing voice for the decentralization of power of Pakistan. As the army was not ready to give in to the political pressure, this led to the secession of East Pakistan (Bangladesh) in 1971 (Dashti 2017).

When the political situation deteriorated in both wings of Pakistan during the 1960s, the army promised to bring reforms in the country through general elections and constitutional changes and transferred power from one general to another in 1969. General Ayub Khan was replaced by General Yahya Khan as the new martial law administrator and the president of Pakistan. With the change of military ruler and the assurance of elections and a civilian government, there was hope that Pakistan might survive and become a modern democratic state, but later it resulted in bloodshed and the departure of the East Wing of Pakistan. However, the one-unit scheme was brought to an end, and general elections were held in December 1970. After three armed conflicts with Pakistan, the Baloch took part in elections. The National Awami Party won the election in Khyber Pakhtunkhwa (North-West Frontier Province) and Balochistan. The Pakistan People's Party won the elections in Sindh and Punjab, and the Awami League became the largest party in the National Assembly, but the Pakistani army refused to allow the Awami League to form the central government. On March 25, 1971, negotiations between Sheikh Mujibur Rahman and President Yahya Khan ended without any solution. When the Awami League saw no future with Pakistan, the leadership opted for the right to self-determination. With the help of India, East Pakistan became Bangladesh on March 26, 1971.

After losing East Pakistan with a humiliating defeat, the army agreed to accept the government of the Pakistan People's Party in Central, Punjab, and Sindh and the National Awami Party formed governments in Balochistan and Khyber Pakhtunkhwa (North-West Frontier Province) on April 28, 1972. The Baloch formed their first elected government in Balochistan after a long political upheaval and three armed conflicts with Pakistan. Mir Ghaus Bakhsh Bizenjo became the governor, and Sardar Ataullah Mengal, the chief minister of Balochistan. It was high time for the Baloch that their representatives were allowed to take charge of their government. There was a hope that after losing half of the country, the army might accept a process for civilian rule in Pakistan, but soon it turned out to be just a dream. The army began to pull the strings of elected governments by using various pretexts to justify its actions. The military establishment in Pakistan and the king of Iran were equally against the nationalist government of Balochistan. Therefore, they blamed the government of Balochistan for conspiring against both countries, Iran and Pakistan. Various allegations were made public to justify the actions they were about to take in Balochistan. The drop scene of this whole saga unfolded on February 10, 1973, when the government of Pakistan claimed that it had found a stock of Soviet guns and ammunition in the Iraqi Embassy in Islamabad intended to reach the Baloch separatists. The accusations were leveled against the government of Balochistan concerning harboring arms and plotting against Iran and Pakistan with the help of the Soviet Union. The nationalist government of Balochistan was dismissed after nine months, and the Baloch leadership was put behind bars (Dashti 2017).

Following the dismissal of the Balochistan government and the imprisonment of prominent Baloch leaders, the fourth episode of the armed conflict began with Pakistan. The resistance movement led by the Balochistan People's Liberation Front (BPLF) intensified, paralyzing communication and transportation between Balochistan and the other parts of Pakistan. The reaction of the Pakistani armed forces against the militants was brutal, disregarding all universal rules of war. The indiscriminate bombardment of the Pakistani army devastated various towns and killed thousands of noncombatants. The Baloch population came under attack from both sides. It is understood that the Iranian king Mohammad Reza not only opposed the nationalist government of Eastern Balochistan but also played a key role in its removal. Neither Pakistan nor Iran was willing to accept a Baloch nationalistic government or stand a long-running rebellion in the region. Therefore, the Shah of Iran sent a strong message to Balochistan by using his air force against the Baloch resistance alongside the Pakistani army. The main aim of both governments was to crush the rebellion before it expanded or reached the western part of Balochistan. The intense bombardment inflicted heavy casualties and destroyed the positions of guerrilla fighters. By 1975, the resistance movement was seriously weakened, but it did manage to operate one way or another until 1977.

While the imprisoned Baloch leaders—Sardar Ataullah Mengal, Mir Ghaus Bakhsh Bizenjo, and Nawab Khair Bakhsh Marri—were facing the so-called Hyderabad conspiracy case on treason charges, their political party, the NAP, was banned. Almost all Baloch and Pashtun nationalist leaders were accused of conspiring against the state of Pakistan. The trial continued for several years and finished with the end of Mr. Zulfikar Ali Bhutto's government. The government of Mr. Bhutto was overthrown by Chief of Army Staff General Zia-ul-Haq on July 5, 1977. Mr. Zulfikar Bhutto was taken into custody and later executed by hanging. The military government of General Zia-ul-Haq took a softer approach to the Baloch issue. He released the Baloch leadership, including other political prisoners of Balochistan, and began further negotiation to settle the differences between the

Baloch and the government of Pakistan. However, the only relief the Baloch nation received from the Zia administration was the dropping of the fabricated cases against the Baloch leaders and releasing of the political prisoners after a devastating war with Pakistan (Dashti 2017).

From General Zia-ul-Haq to General Pervez Musharraf, various governments came to power and went, but the Baloch demand for greater provincial autonomy and rights continued without receiving any sincere attention from the central governments. General Musharraf began to fix the complex affair of Balochistan with Pakistan with mere force of army that triggered the fifth armed conflict with Balochistan in 2004. When the demands for economic, social, and political rights gained momentum during 2005, the Pakistani army decided to eliminate Baloch political leaders. The towering political figure of Nawab Akbar Khan Bugti demanded greater control over the province's resources and opposed more military bases in Balochistan. Thus, his legitimate demands were met with military actions, and he was killed by the Pakistan Army on August 26, 2006. The Baloch nation was appalled by the assassination of their elderly leader, which fueled the ongoing insurgency even further.

The following years were marked with the blood of the Baloch nation, forced disappearances, torture, assassinations, and kill-and-dump policy. Pakistani security forces and their proxy death squads took the lives of thousands of students, politicians, journalists, writers, doctors, and intellectuals. Around 1,200 people were killed during 2009 alone, and more than a thousand went missing. A prominent scholar, writer, and chairman of the Balochi Academy, Mir Jan Muhammad Dashti had received numerous threats from security forces because of his scholarly works, views, and stand for Balochistan. Ultimately, on February 22, 2009, an assassination attempt was made on Mr. Jan Dashti's life. He sustained serious gunshot injuries but fortunately escaped death. A few months later, three political leaders were killed by Pakistan security forces in Makan. Mr. Ghulam Mohammad (the president of Baloch National Movement [BNM]), Lala Muneer, and Sher Muhammad Baloch, who were also leading political figures of Balochistan, were kidnapped from Turbat on April 3, 2009, by the government agencies, and their bodies were found on April 9, 2009, in Murgaap area near Turbat. The bullet-riddled bodies and mass graves of political activists and human rights campaigners continued to surface in every corner of Balochistan.

State-sponsored atrocities had been reported, and concerns were raised by various human rights organizations, including the Human Rights Commission of Pakistan (HRCP), Amnesty International (AI), Human Rights Watch (HRW), and many more. However, except for some international condemnations, no official and tangible action came from the international community. The indiscriminate killing of Baloch people by government agencies and its death squads had widened the gulf between the Baloch and Pakistan. The suffocating military grip on power continued for seven decades. The internal colonial measures, the immense exploitation of Baloch natural resources, and the brutal onslaught on political activities have led to bad blood between Baloch masses and Pakistani rulers.

Pakistan disregarded the tradition, values, cultures, and languages of the Baloch and began to glorify the history and characters of alien invaders who had brought miseries to the region during their occupations. As observed by Dashti (2017), the ignorance and denial of democratic rights began to alienate Pakistan from the masses. The centralized measures, oppressive actions, and unfair treatment of Baloch people, the prohibition of Balochi language from schools and learning centers, the exploitation of natural resources, the state-sponsored settlement of people from other nationalities in Balochistan to bring about a demographic shift, and the Islamization of secular Baloch society have provoked a general feeling among the Baloch people that Pakistan would never become a democratic and modern state where all nations can have their rights and live with dignity and respect. Heeg (2011) pointed out that to understand the Baloch claim of self-determination and the waves of resistance movements from the day of the annexation of Balochistan into Pakistan till now, one has to extensively examine the history of Baloch people and the newborn state of Pakistan. Besides that, one has to also observe the last political arrangements of the British Empire in the Indian subcontinent, as well as the long historical path of Baloch existence and the resistance in the region.

The creation of new states in the subcontinent without taking different nationalities and their territories and historical background into consideration resulted in a long endless political instability. The historical and cultural background of these ethnic groups run for thousands of years in these areas and cannot be ignored. Besides that, the military rulers have been in a complete state of denial regarding the democratic rights of these nations since the creation of Pakistan. The Pakistani rulers have been stressing the solidarity and oneness based on Islamic character rather than a constitutional framework (Baloch 2007). Jan Dashti (1987) observed that there are four provinces remaining in Pakistan after the secession of Bangladesh in 1971. These remaining nations are forced to accept army rule and identify themselves as false Muslim nations. The majority of people who played the most significant role in bringing Pakistan on the map of the world broke away from it because of military behavior that refused to accept the democratic rights of people.

The language of any group or nation is significant for the transfer of their customs, culture, and traditions from one generation to another, but unfortunately, the Balochi language has been banned from being taught even in the primary level in these countries. These countries do not share or respect the democratic values of international standards. Pakistan is ruled by the army with an iron fist, and Iran is governed by a hardline theocratic regime of ayatollahs. In the presence of these brutal regimes, there is no room for the Baloch to exercise their legitimate rights in these countries. The democratic demands of the Baloch people were always dealt with by the strong force of the state. The Baloch have been facing political, economic, and cultural oppression by Pakistan and Iran for decades. The continued oppressive measures of the central governments have triggered the deep-rooted conflict of Baloch nationalism (Dashti 1987).

The Baloch have seen more than seventy years of suffering and the broken promises of Pakistan and the unprecedented scale of exploitation of their natural resources. The Baloch nation has been facing a ghastly campaign of Pakistani armed forces for the last seventy years. The new face of Pakistan has been unfolding for the last fifteen years in the form of forced disappearances and the killing and dumping of Baloch students, intellectuals, and political activists that have reached the point of systematic genocide of the Baloch population. The voice of the Baloch people has been suppressed by both the Pakistan Army and its proxy religious groups. The army and its religious proxies believe that the Baloch are responsible for weakening the defenses of the only holy Muslim nation-state in the world. They genuinely believe that Pakistan is the only hope for the Muslims of the world. For them, demanding democratic and national rights from the national entities constituting Pakistan means an act of treason against the holy country of Pakistan.

One may ask why Pakistan has such a holy duty to fulfill and no responsibility for its people. Well, there are one or two nation-states in the world; but in Pakistan, there is a Muslim nation-state. Some of the nations may have one or more religions, but in Pakistan, there is a religion that has its nation. A country has an army, but in Pakistan, there is an army that has a country. It is widely believed in Pakistan that Allah favored the creation of Pakistan and the country is given by Allah.

THE PRINCIPLE OF INTERNATIONAL INTERVENTION AND THE BALOCH RIGHT OF SELF-DETERMINATION

The theory and practice of one state or a group of states intervening militarily into another country to put an end to the human rights violations and protect people from being harmed by their state are called international interventions. The principle of humanitarian intervention is based on the notion of protecting people from being harmed. The actions of a consistent case of human rights violations of a state would transfer the duty of the protection to the broader community, which is to the international community. Thereby, the international humanitarian intervention law outweighs the notion of nonintervention in the affairs of a sovereign state. Many actions of the religious fundamentalist states of Pakistan and Iran during the last few decades are in clear violation of international laws concerning the protection of citizens. This chapter is an analysis of the concept of international intervention in context, and it will relate the doctrine of international intervention with the continuous and blatant violations of the fundamental human rights of the Baloch people.

The International Intervention

The term *humanitarian intervention* has a broad meaning that contains a wide range of actions taken by a state or states to protect people from violence or improve their conditions of well-being across state borders. In other words, it is the actions carried out by the international community to protect the political, social, and economic rights of the individuals. Thus, it is understood that human beings did not face the viciousness of the rulers because of the lack of laws and moral principles, but they suffered because of the bad deeds of their masters who were unwilling to be restrained by any rules. The universal human rights principles state that it is the duty of all states to promote and protect human rights regardless of their political and economic issues. In the last few decades, the internationally recognized human rights rules have gained huge support throughout the world. From a practical point of view, humanitarian intervention may also take place through peaceful means if the country of particular concern submits to international pressure and allows the international observers and peacekeeping force into the country.

The Historical Background

The theory of human rights was derived from the ancient Greek political philosophy of the polis (city-state) and its privilege of citizenship. The idea of humanitarian intervention was advanced by various legal and political philosophers much later in human history. It became part of legal and political debate in Europe around the sixteenth century. During its early times, the humanitarian intervention rule was based on natural moral principles. The philosophy of modern natural law evolved in the Age of Enlightenment, challenging the divine right of kings and establishing the social contract and positive law of governments.

During the period spanning from sixteenth to twentieth century, many scholars and legal and political philosophers—such as Hugo

Grotius, Samuel von Pufendorf, Emer de Vattel, and John Locke—debated a wide spectrum of the law of nations. Their international legal methods are the foundation of contemporary international principles. Hugo Grotius (1583–1645) introduced a political and moral standard of humanitarian intervention principle, relating it to state sovereignty and international relations. In his just war theory, he emphasized that the war can be justified on the ground of protecting human beings from tyranny. He believed that a community benefits from the rule of law so the nations can be harmonized under certain international principles. Emer de Vattel (1714–1767) published his legal theory, *The Law of Nations or, Principles of the Law of Nature, Applied to the Conduct and Affairs of Nations and Sovereigns*, in 1758. He examined the rules of law governing the conduct of sovereign states and nations. His concept of international law was greatly admired during the seventeenth to nineteenth century. The influential philosopher John Locke (1632–1704) also observed the nature of free man in his *Two Treatises of Government*. He defined the legal rights to life and liberty in a just society where men are free and equal and entrust some of their rights to the government to establish a comfortable society where they all enjoy their lives and liberty. He stated that if a government fails to protect the rights and liberty of its citizens, then that government should be replaced by its people.

Despite having moral and legal rules and the desire for an international system to protect human beings from the barbaric rulers of the world, this only became a reality in the nineteenth century when the European nations adopted humanitarian intervention as part of international legal norms. However, the justifying criteria of international intervention stand the same as a state waging war and crossing the line of an international border or committing a crime against humanity or failing to fulfill its responsibility as a state.

The United Nations and International Intervention

The world was shocked by Nazi Germany killing six million Jews during the Second World War. The reaction of the world was immediate in terms of adopting the Genocide Convention and embracing the Universal Declaration of Human Rights (UDHR) in 1948, promising protection of people and individuals across the world.

The adoption of the convention was a milestone in the development of human rights in the contemporary world. The internationalization of the world's peace and security and ambition for a new method of protection of inalienable human rights has greatly changed global politics. The declaration provided a collective and international response to the rights of individuals, and it was asserted that human rights would have primacy over the sovereignty of the state. For the first time in history, states came under the direct scrutiny of the international community and the nongovernmental organizations about their domestic conduct. The United Nations set out the power of states and international legal norms through its chapters 6 and 7 of the Security Council, which became responsible for the world's peace and security (Kochler 2001).

The universal declaration was followed by various international conventions and legal methods, bringing the human rights issue into the heart of international organizations. However, the Western values of democracy and human rights fell in the web of a legal and moral debate of state sovereignty and nonintervention rule, which used to be a pretext for rogues and the most abusive regimes. In other words, the rule of so-called territorial integrity was a license to kill as long as the killings were committed within the state boundaries. The dilemma for the modern world was to choose between human life and the border of states. According to the international legal order, the essential responsibility of human rights protection of the citizens lies within the state, but human life and the protection of internationally recognized legal norms were more important than the borders of some rogue states. Therefore, it was stated that if states violate their responsibility of protection or fail to respond to gross human rights abuses within their boundaries, the international obligation to protect human rights will be invoked and the state in breach of international law will face international condemnation and force (Abiew 1999).

States are considered equal members of the international community and enjoy equal rights to maintain their various affairs. They also have equal duties for the entire community of nations and are expected to guarantee human rights and dignity. The obligation of a state regarding the rights of its citizens is considered to be part of its statehood and sovereignty. The sovereignty of a state is not holy per se; it is the people who make a state respectful. A responsible and modern state means a state having a just system respecting the democratic rights of its people according to international legal orders. Sovereignty of a state is important so that the rights of its people are the source of the legitimacy of the state.

Humanitarian intervention is a form of collective reaction of the international community against the violation of its core principles. The common standards of human rights and dignity are essential for maintaining friendly relations among all nations. The universal nature of rights cannot be ignored or overlooked by the modern world, as they are shared principles and equally valued by all. Because of that, the violation of international human rights norms may trigger outrage among the international community, and the responsible state would face the consequences. The international community may use force against a state to halt violence against a civilian. However, it is reluctant to use force against abusive regimes until it is necessary. There is a tendency to use peaceful means first to reach out to those suffering under a cruel regime, but if the peaceful methods do not work, then the use of force can be enforced (Orford 2003).

The peaceful method of UN operations is designed to ease the tension, monitor the situation, and provide an environment for negotiation. The humanitarian access mission can be deployed on request or with the consent of the state in conflict or without consent or request. Thus, if a state is unable to protect or guarantee the rights of its people, then there is an international community that has to make sure that people have access to a just system. However, as observed by Abiew (1999), despite the adoption of the Genocide Convention, the creation of the International Court of Justice, and the development of the principle of humanitarian intervention, the international community has failed to prevent genocide and systematic mass slaughter in many parts of the world.

By the end of the Second World War, new states began to appear on the map of the world, carrying with them long-running disputes, divisions, and the complex legacy of their colonizers who had ruled over them for hundreds of years. During their ruling era, the colonizers used every means available to divide and conquer; therefore, on their departure, they left behind their legacy of ethnic, tribal, religious, cultural, and political upheavals for newborn states around the globe. While the new states grappled with postcolonial issues, the division of their society widened, which led to regional wars among different ethnic, religious, and political groups in different parts of the world. Some of the newborn states disintegrated even further after gaining independence from the colonial powers, and many of them are still going through wars and political instability (Abiew 1999).

After the formation of the United Nations, there were two waves of international interventions occurring during the Cold War and in the post–Cold War. In 1960–1964, Belgium and the United States intervened in the Congo after violence broke out in the country, which was followed by US interventions in the Dominican Republic in 1965, Grenada in 1983, and Panama in 1989. France and Belgium intervened in Zaire in 1978, and in the same year, Vietnam launched an attack on Cambodia. France has intervened in the Central African Republic seven times since its independence in 1960. Alongside the above interventions, one of the most significant humanitarian interventions took place in South Asia during the disintegration of Pakistan in 1971. The systematic genocide committed by the Pakistani army in East Pakistan (now Bangladesh) prompted Indians to act, and the Indian Army intervened, preventing further slaughter of the Bengali, which was one of the worst genocides in modern history. The second wave of interventions came after the dissolution of the Soviet Union in 1991, which was more collective in terms of international norms and organization.

The Collapse of the Soviet Union

During the Cold War, the United Nations was partially paralyzed by the geopolitical rivalry of the two great powers of the Soviet Union and the United States. They competed for influence in the developing world and beyond, keeping the world divided between two political ideologies of communism and capitalism for more than forty years. However, the collapse of the Soviet Union was one of the biggest events in the twentieth century, which brought drastic changes in the political arena of the world. International power remained in the hands of Western powers led by the United States. The United Nations began to move alongside the United States, North Atlantic Treaty Organization (NATO), and the Western allied forces with a new approach for the world's peace and security. At the same time, the world was engulfed by numerous devastating conflicts from Africa to Europe and beyond (Orford 2003).

The collapse of the Soviet Union in the 1990s resulted in fifteen sovereign states, which were followed by Yugoslavia and Czechoslovakia. Yugoslavia split into six countries, and Czechoslovakia divided into two states of the Czech Republic and Slovakia. It was followed by numerous conflicts in Africa and beyond. When the barriers of East-West went down, the demand for humanitarian intervention in the conflict zones faced less resistance in the United Nations. The protection of democratic rights of individuals gained international recognition, and the states came under immense pressure concerning their human rights issues.

The UN was urged to take immediate action and not to get lost in the perennial debate of legal, illegal, moral, and immoral deeds of international law when the human beings are going through devastating wars and suffering. The safeguarding of international measures of human rights were considered to be the best legal virtues of the modern world. The involvement of the United Nations rapidly increased in international politics, particularly in the humanitarian issues of the world. On various occasions, the Security Council agreed and authorized humanitarian intervention; and in some other times, the intervention went ahead without the UN mandate, which was a positive change in the behavior of the international community toward the protection of universal human rights. The leading force of the United States and NATO led various humanitarian interventions in different parts of the world with the support of the UN. A new chapter of humanitarian intervention opened, increasing the United Nations peacekeeping missions during the 1990s (Murphy 1996).

As the world connected through an information revolution, the media captured the attention of the entire world by televising the unimaginable suffering of people in war-torn countries, which had never been possible before. The darkest spots of the world were exposed to the international audience. The graphic pictures of brutality, massacre, bombardment, and scattered dead bodies of women and children have shaken the consciousness of people around the globe. The response to these mixed conflicts of civil war and grave human rights violations and persecution was the result of the increasing pressure from people and nongovernmental organizations to protect civilians from widespread human rights abuses by their governments (Orford 2003).

The Economic Community of West African States (ECOWAS) sent their peacekeeping mission to Liberia in 1990 to monitor the situation in the war-torn country, but when the country descended into chaos even further, it obligated the UN-NATO forces (UNMIL) to intervene in 2003. In 1991, the United States, France, and the United Kingdom established a no-fly zone in northern Iraq to protect the Kurdish population from Saddam's attacks, as he had already massacred thousands of Kurds with chemical attacks. The United States also became part of international humanitarian efforts in Somalia in 1992, as the situation exacerbated further, which was followed by the US intervention in Haiti in 1994, following the coup d'état of 1991. The mission for Rwanda was established by the UN Security Council on October 5, 1993, and the intervention was authorized by the United Nations. The UN-led mission for Sierra Leone (UNAMSIL), which deployed in 1999, was followed by the intervention of the United Kingdom on May 7, 2000. The conflict of Yugoslavia triggered the NATO bombing of Yugoslavia on March 24, 1999, which led to the withdrawal of the Yugoslavian army from Kosovo. After that, the United Nations established the United Nations Interim Administration Mission in Kosovo. On March 19, 2011, a multistate NATO-led intervention in Libya brought down the regime of Colonel Gaddafi who ruled over Libya for four decades and was still roaring that he would show no mercy for the people who were demanding political reforms. Besides the above humanitarian interventions, the United Nations played a great part in the independence of Eritrea in 1991, East Timor in 1999, and South Sudan in 2011 (Weiss 2012).

All these humanitarian interventions were triggered by inhuman actions of a cruel ruler, regime, dictator, and warlords; and sadly, the majority of them have escaped justice. However, since then there has been a great shift in the international justice system, the International Court of Justice has managed to bring some of those criminals to justice through its numerous tribunals. The International Criminal Tribunal for the former Yugoslavia (ICTY) was established in 1993, which dealt with crimes committed during the Balkans conflict in the 1990s. Similar tribunals were created for Rwanda (1994), Cambodia (1997), East Timor (2000), and Sierra Leone (2002). The international community has been asserting its position by the internationalization of human rights. For the first time in human history, people have realized that the universal principle of human rights was not a mere good expression for humanity. At last, it was serving the interests of a human being to some extent. The new adoption of the Responsibility to Protect in 2005 gave the United Nations and its associate groups, like US and NATO, more power to act faster in the need for immediate response (Hehir 2010).

The world was a different place when the Universal Declaration of Human Rights was adopted in 1948. Since then, there have been numerous significant human rights conventions addressing all issues of protective measures. Despite the difficulties, delays, weaknesses, and failures in many cases, the methods of international humanitarian intervention have greatly helped humanity across the globe. However, there is still a long way to go, as many nations and groups are facing subjugation, suppression, persecution, internal colonialism, and systematic genocide in the twenty-first century. The Baloch are among those nations seeking international intervention in the face of genocide by the religious state of Pakistan.

International Intervention and Balochistan

The Baloch faced some of the worst subjugation, persecution, and genocide throughout their long history. Ironically, these modern waves of atrocities have begun in the same year when the great convention of human rights (UDHR) was adopted in the United Nations. Balochistan was invaded by Pakistan on the pretext of making a Muslim nation-state in South Asia after its creation by the departing British Empire in 1947. Countries and nations are not born overnight like Pakistan—without a land, history, nation, language, and culture, meaning no legal and moral grounding for Pakistan. Yet it was allowed to invade the thousand-year-old nation-state of Balochistan. The invasion of Pakistan on March 27, 1948, became the darkest day of the Baloch history, and it has been getting darker for the last seventy-two years.

As Pakistan sought a more tangible base of unity and identity after its sudden creation, it drifted under the boots of the army without having a chance of realizing its locality. When the army realized that it had a country in the name of a Muslim nation without any challenge from political leadership, it began to rule over Pakistan using Islam as the core unifying force of the country. The Islamization of Pakistan resulted in a military-mullah state. The dreams of a new state for Muslims becoming a federal democracy died down fast. On the other hand, the Baloch was already a Muslim nation and did not need to join a new nation to become more Muslim than they were. However, the rejection of joining the Allah-given state of Pakistan made the Baloch sinners in the eyes of Pakistan's military establishment. Since the Pakistani incursion into Balochistan in 1948, the Baloch people have been the prime target of Pakistan's state machinery. As soon as Balochistan was conquered, the government of Pakistan adopted a policy of excluding the Baloch people from the power structure of the country and denied their political, economic, and social rights, which became the focal point of the long-running conflict between the Baloch and the state of Pakistan.

The Baloch resisted politically, and with five armed resistances, the colonial designs of the religious state. The new phase of insurgency in Balochistan has begun with the assassination of Nawab Akbar Khan Bugti by the Pakistani army in 2006. The brutal murder of the eighty-year-old Baloch leader outraged the whole nation, which was followed by targeted murders of Baloch political and intellectual personalities. They were eliminated because they were campaigning for the political rights of the Baloch people and were raising voices for the release of thousands of missing persons from Balochistan.

The Country of Missing Persons

The first and most important role of a state is to protect its citizens from being harmed, and the second is to provide them with justice according to laws of the state and rules of the international legal orders. But in Pakistan, things are very different, perhaps because Pakistan is not a normal country. Let alone protecting or providing the means of justice, Pakistan is causing injuries and slaughtering its citizens. The only reason for that is that they dare to question the draconian policy of the state or demand their democratic rights. On the other hand, the Islamic extremists, Taliban, and other outlaws enjoy freedom of activity. They are allowed to incite and carry out violent acts against liberal politicians, human rights activists, and the minorities groups. The army consider them part of the sacred security forces of the Allah-given state. On various occasions, the Inter-Services Intelligence (ISI) of Pakistan called these jihadi groups strategic assets of the state.

The present phase of atrocities on the Baloch started when the army began a devastating military campaign against the Baloch national resistance during the reign of General Musharraf. The army was joined by its proxy jihadi organizations that unleashed a reign of terror throughout Balochistan. Numerous death squads were created by intelligence agencies. They are assisting the military establishment in its dirty works of dumping the bodies of political activists in remote areas of Balochistan. Many of the jihadi organizations patronized by the army are believed to be harboring international terrorists who have carried out many acts of terrorism in countries, including France, the United States, the United Kingdom, and India. The Allah-given country has become a haven or heaven for terrorists. It became hell for those who are raising voices for their national rights or opposing the exploitation of their natural resources. It became the worst place on this planet earth for human rights campaigners and religious minorities.

When the phenomenon of enforced disappearances began to unfold in Balochistan, people took to the streets protesting against the arbitrary arrests of students and political activists. The voices of human rights organizations, political leaders, and protesters were met with yet with more abductions and disappearances. To add insult to injury, the people who took part in the protests for the release of missing persons were abducted and made missing persons too. The situation deteriorated even further when the security forces began to target those who simply expressed their thoughts about the harsh policy of the state toward the Baloch nation. The military crackdown on freedom of expression reached alarming levels when speaking about the military actions and Balochistan became a military created taboo. The media was also banned from reporting about missing persons or the mutilated dead bodies that were constantly resurfacing in every corner of Balochistan.

The armed forces have been using heavy artillery and helicopter gunships against the Baloch people. These indiscriminate attacks on civilian settlements have caused heavy civilian casualties, including women and children, in many parts of Balochistan. In some cases, entire towns and villages were burned down by the army, making thousands of internally displaced persons (IDP). Thousands of people have been missing for years, and their fate is still unknown. These barbaric actions against the population are designed to silence the resilient voice of Balochistan. There is strong evidence that the continued forced disappearances and the kill-and-dump policy of Pakistan have become a systematic genocide of the Baloch nation. These heinous crimes against humanity have been widely reported by many national and international organizations, including Pakistan Human Rights Commission, Amnesty International, and Human Rights Watch.

As observed by Murswiek (1993), those regimes that are involved in depriving people of their specific characters are in breach of all human rights conventions under international law. For example, the prohibition of speaking their language and banning it from the education system, destroying the basis of their distinct existence as an ethnic group; the undesirable expulsion of a part of the population from their territory by force or creating a situation for causing such movement or moving and positioning another group of people from the other part of the country to outnumber the people in their territory; and the imprisonment or execution of the group leaders are blatant violations of self-determination and human rights (Murswiek 1993). Pakistan and Iran are among the worst human rights violators in modern history, and they are equally responsible for sponsoring jihadists in various countries. Both states are too far from becoming responsible members of the international community. They are involved in massive human rights violations and unable to interact and function with the modern world. The behavior of these countries is disastrous and may be a great threat to the world's peace and security.

Essentially, human rights protection is the prime responsibility of every state. However, when a state refuses to accept internationally recognized human rights values or fails to protect the basic human rights of its citizens or a state descends into a civil war and is unable to protect people from violence, it becomes the responsibility of the civilized world to intervene. This intervention can be military and peaceful. The international rules cover all humanity—regardless of their country, race, and religion—fighting for their inalienable right to lead a life free from persecution. The world leaders have been asserting time and time again that the fundamental principle of humanity must triumph in our new emerging world. The concept of a humanitarian intervention lies in the moral and legal responsibility of the international community, and the international legal system must not be hijacked by the bureaucratic rules and regulations while human lives are at stake. Searching for a flawless international legal approach would give us thousands of dead bodies and catastrophic human suffering. Safeguarding the lives of people should be the core of the international principle of intervention, not some legal technicalities. The international community has a responsibility to protect those facing grave human rights violations such as the Baloch in Pakistan and Iran. The people of Balochistan have been suffering for too long, and both these states have failed to accommodate the issues of Balochistan. Therefore, international humanitarian intervention in Balochistan is the only option to bring an end to the miseries of Baloch people and provide them with the long waiting promise to determine their destiny.

Despite the recognition of the right of self-determination as a human right and a legally binding international law, many colonial successors states have been getting away without facing any serious consequences for their actions against the right of people. The slow and ineffective role of the United Nations has raised serious questions about its will or ability to enforce international law. As the responsibility of a state, the rules of international law and the huge duty of the United Nations toward people are clear about human rights violations. Therefore, the failure of any state from meeting its obligation regarding human rights should be considered an immediate call for the UN's involvement in the matter concerned. The UN, ICJ, and the international community have to find more operational ways to enforce international legal orders. It is understood that the right of self-determination and the so-called territorial integrity cannot be practiced at the same time. It has been adopted in the UN Charter that the rights and the protection of people must prevail over the state authority.

A modern state with a developed institutional system of social justice within and playing its rule according to international norms is in the interest of the international community; therefore, no one wishes to weaken its position. But at the same time, if the state is unable to do its duties, there come the international legal methods to do the legitimate work for the new world. These international measures are often taken to resolve the long-running conflicts around the globe. In some conflicts, the only way to peace and stability is the disintegration of the state concerned (Murswiek 1993).

The idea of giving people the right to self-determination is to provide them with a political condition in which they can build their social and cultural values in their historical territory, enjoy complete freedom, and develop their identity as an ethnic group. The right of self-determination and secession is an integral part of international law. In some political disputes, giving of autonomy to the group concerned may help to ease the crisis if it is applied in the true equal sense of democracy in the existing state. Nondemocratic states fear that granting autonomy to these groups will open the door for secession and, ultimately, to the disintegration of the state. The international legal experts think otherwise; they believe if people are given their democratic right equally and granted autonomy to decide their local matters, this helps to build a strong state. Autonomy may prevent a state from breaking off if it is acknowledged on time, but if the demand for autonomy is not accepted on in its early call, then demand for secession will intensify and separation shall be inevitable.

C H A P T E R

TEN

CONCLUSION

The ambitions of the European powers changed the shape of the world during their colonial era. They went from one corner of the world to another conquering continents, countries, and nations. They divided nations and their countries and changed their way of life in various ways forever. Therefore, on their departure after the Second World War, they left behind far-reaching disputes and divisions among many nations and groups in different parts of the world. The most damaging divisions were made by the British Empire in Africa and South Asia.

Religion became a crucial weapon for the British to divide the Indian subcontinent. The peace-loving people of India lived in harmony for thousands of years with their different religious belief systems. The British Raj used religion mercilessly, and the administration brought out religious dogma from the temple and mosque into politics, breaking the bond of the Indian community. It is believed that besides the power of British artillery, it was the policy of divide and rule that made it possible for a small number of British officials and troops to rule over hundreds of millions of Indians for almost two hundred years. Some of these divisions and disputes were carried forward in the newly emerging states for future strategic leverage, and these issues are still instrumental for the former colonial powers in many parts of the world.

With the end of the Second World War in 1945, the British Empire began to crumble. On the one hand, the process of decolonization brought hope and freedom for various nations; but on the other hand, it brought destruction and disputes in many parts of the world. The most disastrous event took place in South Asia, where an artificial state was designed. A country was created without having a nation, land, language, culture, and historical background in the Indian subcontinent. Present-day Pakistan was carved out of India merely in the name of religion, and this new country for a so-called Muslim nation was generously bestowed with the homeland of numerous nations by the sinking British Empire. The lands of those historical nations were simply gifted away to the newborn state of Pakistan because they were located in the region where Pakistan was being planned by Great Britain. The creation of Pakistan and the support of the Muslim Brotherhood in different parts of the world paved the way for a growing radical Islamic ideology that has been glorifying a holy war since then. They were given a sense of identifying themselves with religion instead of their nationality and ethnic groups. It was all done to dilute the nationalistic sentiment in the colonized world. The creation of Pakistan along religious lines opened the doors for unending religious conflict in South Asia and beyond.

Along with other nations, the Baloch woke up one morning to find themselves living in a place called Pakistan. After three thousand years of their history and existence in their homeland, Balochistan was invaded by Pakistan on March 27, 1948. Since the invasion of Balochistan, Pakistani rulers have been completely ignoring the history, tradition, culture, and languages of the Baloch and the other nations in Pakistan. The people of Pakistan have been forced to accept a bizarre and peculiar theory of a Muslim nation for more than seven decades and the grip of a suffocating military junta on power.

As one of the oldest nations in the region, the Baloch refused to submit to the odd theory of Muslims being a nation. They refused to forget their history, land, language, and thousands of years of existence. Thereby, the Baloch and Balochistan became the prime target of the military establishment of Pakistan. The people of Balochistan have been suffering for so long at the hands of the Pakistani armed forces and its proxy religious groups. Since the forcible annexation of Balochistan into Pakistan, the relationship between the Baloch and Pakistani rulers has been a shaky one. The people of Balochistan have been seeking recognition as a nation within Pakistan for decades; therefore, they have participated in the governing bodies of Pakistan, hoping to build a federal democratic country where all nations of Pakistan could enjoy equal rights. But the tragedy of Pakistan is that the country has never got a chance to develop a civilian system of democracy and no nationalities have been allowed to freely choose their representatives since the creation of Pakistan. It is ruled by a misguided army that tends to change its colors of rule at times by disguising itself as a civilian administration. While displaying the face of a civilian government, the army hires or chooses a bunch of its loyal people as the representatives of people of Pakistan and they run the show for some time before being sent home. This has been the game with Pakistan since it was separated from India.

All these colors of army rule and actions generally against the democratic values in Pakistan and particularly the several brazen military operations in Balochistan triggered a strong nationalistic sentiment among the Baloch masses who have never forgotten their enforced assimilation into Pakistan. Ultimately, the Baloch have come to realize that Pakistani rulers would not allow the country to become a modern multinational state where all nations can live together in peace and with respect. Therefore, the demand of the Baloch people for democracy and more autonomy gradually shifted into the right to self-determination. This significant right is enshrined in the legal order of the international community, and all states have a responsibility to respect the will of the people. The fact of the matter is that a claim of right to self-determination is aligned with all democratic rights people enjoy in their states. This is a human right and also a legal principle of international law.

The concept of self-determination is widely known and expressed but rarely understood in terms of its legal character in the international arena. It is all about granting people the right to choose freely their economic, social, and cultural rights through international legal methods. It was one of the greatest aims of the 1945 Charter of the United Nations. It came as the first right in the human rights covenants of 1966 and also as one of the foundation rules of the

Friendly Relations Declaration of 1970. It has been considered as the backbone of peace, security, and human rights in the Helsinki Final Act of 1975.

In the contemporary world, all states should adopt a constitutional framework that grants the right of self-determination according to the will of people. The concept of sovereignty comes with great responsibility and restrictions. The jurisdiction of the power of a state and the right to self-determination go hand in hand. Thus, the state may exercise its internal and external matters to some extent; but when it comes to dealing with other countries or a case of rights of people, the internationally recognized state responsibilities come under the universal system of the modern world. The rules of international law addressing the right of self-determination go through the heart of human rights and dignity.

The issue of the right of self-determination is rarely invoked in developed countries. It does not mean that all these developed countries are one-nation states and do not have any issues among different groups. The simple explanation is that they have developed a just governing system, sharing power among all nationalities, and they are in great harmony and think that they are stronger and better off together. But the situation in the developing world is vice versa. Let alone a just system, they are ruled by a family, a group of elite, army, and theocracy. The rulers cannot allow a just governing system for their people because that would mean losing their authority. These kinds of totalitarian regimes rule over their countries with an iron fist. That's why they are plagued with economic, social, and cultural problems. Instead of bringing all stakeholders of the country on board and addressing the issues of the state, they tend to use oppressive measures to curb the democratic demands of people. Oppressive policy always leads to a deepening division in society and will not hold for too long. Demands such as for self-determination will not cease because of the draconian policy of a government. It can only cease by addressing the true nature of it and arranging some kind of constitutional methods to ease the tension between the governments and the people concerned.

There are countries, such as Pakistan and Iran, that do not have respect for human rights and believe that they are above international laws and they can deny any legitimate demands of people by force and subjugation. The history of multinational countries shows that people of different groups will not accept a forced arrangement of a state in this manner. People tend to identify themselves with their common history, culture, land, language, myth, and shared origin. If these elements of people are rejected and they are forced to accept the identity of their oppressor, then you are going to face a growing conflict.

The international community and international legal experts agreed that those countries that do not handle their internal matters of human rights according to the international rules and that use suppressive measures should face immediate consequences. Human rights cannot and should not differ from place to place, and the UN has a huge responsibility to make it true. The UN and the international community have a significant role to play in the world: maintaining peace and security and protecting the rights of people from oppressive regimes. In those countries that do not protect the rights of their people, international methods of protection of human rights should intervene, bringing the suppressive states under international law. It is observed that if people are given democratic rights to decide their future, then the claim such as the right to self-determination can be resolved without going through this destructive and painful phase. But if the people are constantly denied their democratic rights, the eruption of violence would be inevitable. In the case of such unfolding conflicts, international intervention and response have to be immediate in order to minimize the scale of violence and bloodshed.

The protection of the right of all peoples to self-determination is the fundamental principle of international law that constitutes an *erga omnes* under the obligation of all states to ensure that the universal rights of people are respected. The denial or breach of this most important rule of the community, particularly through the use of force, is considered to be a serious breach of international law. The principle defines not just the responsibilities of states regarding respect for human rights but also prohibits the use of any kind of force that may deprive people of enjoying such rights. The use of force against people who simply want to exercise their legitimate rights is illegal, strongly condemned by the international community, and punishable through the International Court of Justice.

Sometimes there is a conflict between a group on one side claiming the right of self-determination and on the other side a state claiming to hold absolute sovereignty on its territory. In these kinds of situations, the solution has to be found through various international legal means bearing in mind the commitment to protecting and promoting human rights. Human rights are the key to the implementation of self-determination. The development and recognition of self-determination has been one of the greatest virtues of the international community to uproot subjugation and oppression of people by states. The human rights were adopted by the international community to promote and protect rights globally through a legally binding framework. They were recognized in international treaties and documents. The right of self-determination is reaching out to those who are suffering from subjugation, exploitation, and systematic oppression by state or groups.

The self-determination and human rights principles are inseparable and have become partners in various international declarations and covenants—for instance, in the International Human Rights Covenant of 1966; the International Covenant on Economic, Social and Cultural Rights; and the International Covenant on Civil and Political Rights. These rules were adopted by the United Nations and should have been enforced since 1976. Self-determination also has been defined in regional instruments as a principle of international law in the Final Act of the Conference on Security and Cooperation in Europe (CSCE) 1975 and in the African Charter on Human and Peoples' Right (1981). Furthermore, the jurists argue that the right of self-determination is the legal part of jus cogens and that it's now a demonstrable international human rights law of our contemporary world. The right of self-determination is vital for promoting and protecting human rights globally; thereby, the United Nations have acknowledged in both of its covenants, ICCPR and ICESCR, that self-determination is a part of positive international legal method. The empowerment of people and groups is at the core of human rights. Giving rights to people to decide their matters is the best way to protect them from being dehumanized and oppressed by their governments.

The right to self-determination is a crucial legal principle for the protection of people from rogue states and yet the most compromised international rule in the name of so-called state sovereignty. Surely there are some guarantees for the sovereignty of weak and smaller states, but those assurances cannot be a shield for crimes against their people or actions threatening the peace and security of the world.

No state in any circumstances should be allowed to use its power to deprive people of their democratic and inalienable rights. The United Nations is the last hope and remedy for millions on our planet earth. Despite its weakness and failures, it has been a great resort for solving disputes and conflicts of states and nations around the globe. The United Nations' involvement in the case of East Timor, Eritrea, Kosovo, South Sudan, and other parts of the world brought freedom and peace for those people.

The Baloch demand for the right of self-determination has legal foundations. The protection of basic human rights became essential to the state's role in the international arena, and the transgression of its international duties regarding vital human rights makes it an unfit member of the international community. The preservation and existence of people as ethnic groups and their democratic rights are no threat to a state's sovereignty or territorial integrity. The respect and guarantee of those rights of people will enhance the role of the state in the wider community as a responsible partner in international politics. In other words, statehood comes from the people it represents in the name of a country, state, or government. When a state fails to perform its international obligations about human rights abuses and carries on its unjust behavior, endangering the existence of the group concerned, it shall justify and legitimize their demand for secession from the state they live in. The democratic rights of people are the key to their survival and existence with others, and it is the duty of the state to make sure that these rights are realized. The protection of their political rights—including language, culture, and social fabric—is the responsibility of the state.

Immediate actions should be taken for those people who are facing grave human rights violations in their states, like the Baloch in Pakistan and Iran. It is the collective duty of the international community to make sure that the Baloch nation receives attention and justice. Besides the United Nations, the United Kingdom—as the heir to the former colonial power—also bears some moral and legal responsibilities toward the people of Balochistan.

REFERENCES

Abiew, K. F. 1999. *The Evolution of the Doctrine and Practice of Humanitarian Intervention*. Edited by Francis Kofi Abiew. Kluwer Law International.

Accessed April 25, 2018. http://www.bbc.co.uk/history/british/modern/partition1947_01.shtml.

Accessed 2/11/2018. http://www.un.org/en/peacekeeping/missions/unmis/background.shtml.

Addison, P. 1975. *The Road to 1945: British Politics and the Second World War*. Jonathan Cape Ltd.

Ahmed, S. 2004. *Bangladesh: Past and Present*. New Delhi: APH Publishing Co.

Amnesty International. 2007. Iran: *Human Rights Abuses against the Baluchi Minority*. London: Amnesty International Secretariat.

Ballard, R. J. 2008. *Triumph of Self-Determination: Operation Stabilise and United Nations Peacemaking in East Timor*. Greenwood Publishing Group.

Baloch, I. 1987. *The Problem of Greater Baluchistan: A Study of Baluch Nationalism*. Stuttgart: Steiner Verlag Wiesbaden GMBH.

Baloch, S. 2007. *In a Baloch Perspective*. Edited by N. Dashti. Quetta: Asaap Publication.

Bass, J. G. 2013. *The Blood Telegram: Nixon, Kissinger, and a Forgotten Genocide*. Alfred A. Knopf.

Bates, C. 2011. *The Hidden Story of Partition and Its Legacies*.

Baxter, C. 1998. *Bangladesh: From a Nation to a State*. New York: Perseus.

BBC. 2013. Available at http://www.bbc.co.uk/news/world-africa-14069082 (South Sudan).

Besenyo, J. 2009. *Western Sahara*. Publikon Publisher.

Besson, S., and J. d'Aspremont, eds. 2017. *The Oxford Handbook of the Sources of International Law*. Oxford University Press.

Brownlie, I. 2008. *International Law: Seventh Edition*. Oxford University Press.

Buchanan, A. 2003. *Justice, Legitimacy, and Self-Determination: Moral Foundations of International Law*. Oxford: Oxford University Press.

Cambridge University Press.

Carter, A. 2009. "Gandhi and the Literature on Non-Violent Resistance." In *Civil Resistance and Power Politics: The Experience of Non-Violent Action from Gandhi to the Present*, edited by A. Roberts and T. G. Ash. Oxford University Press.

Cassese, A. 1995.

Castellino, J. 2014. "International Law and Self-Determination." In Christian

Choudhury, G. W. 1972. *Bangladesh: Why It Happened* 48, no. 2. Royal Institute of International Affairs.

Copnall, J. 2014. *A Poisonous Thorn in Our Hearts: Sudan and South Sudan's Bitter and Incomplete Divorce*. C. Hurst and Co. Publishers.

Daly, M. W. 1991. *Imperial Sudan: The Anglo-Egyptian Condominium 1934–1956*. Cambridge University Press.

Dashti, Jan. 1982. *The Baloch Cultural Heritage*. Karachi: Royal Book Company.

Dashti, Jan. 1989. *Essays on Baloch National Struggle in Pakistan: Emergence, Dimensions, Repercussions*. Quetta: Gosha e Adab.

Dashti, Jan., ed. 2007. *In a Baloch Perspective*. Edited by N. Dashti. Quetta: Asaap Publication.

Dashti, N. 2012. *The Baloch and Balochistan: A Historical Account from the Beginning to the Fall of the Baloch State*. Bloomberg: Trafford Publishing.

Dashti, N. 2017. *The Baloch Conflict with Iran and Pakistan: Aspects of a National Liberation Struggle*. Bloomberg: Trafford Publishing.

Dashti, N., ed. 2007. *In a Baloch Perspective*. Quetta: Asaap Publication.

Degan, V. D. 1997. *Sources of International Law*. Martnus Nijhoff Publishers.

Deng, F. M. 1995. *War of Visions: Conflict of Identities in Sudan*. Washington, DC: Brookings Institution.

Dworkin, G. 1988. *The Theory of Practice of Autonomy*. Cambridge University Press.

Eriksen, H. T. 1993. *Ethnicity and Nationalism: Anthropological Perspectives*. London: Pluto Press.

Gankovsky, Y. V. 1971. *The Peoples of Pakistan*. Moscow: Nauka.

Gellner, E. 2006. *Nations and Nationalism, Second Edition*. Oxford: Blackwell Publishing Ltd.

Grotius, H. 2018. *On the Law of War and Peace*. Jazzybee Verlag.

Gunn, G. C. 2010. *Historical Dictionary of East Timor*. Scarecrow Press.

Hail, S. 1988. "The Historical Background to the Ethiopia-Eritrea Conflict." In *The Long Struggle of Eritrea for Independence and Constructive Peace*, edited by L. Cliffe and B. Davidson. Red Sea Press Inc.

Hannum, H. 1990. *Autonomy, Sovereignty and Self-Determination: The Accommodation of Conflicting Rights (Procedural Aspects of International Law)*. University of Pennsylvania Press.

Harrison, S. 1981. *In Afghanistan's Shadow: Baluch Nationalism and Soviet Temptations*. New York: Carnegie Endowment for International Peace.

Heeg, J. 2011. *Insurgency in Balochistan*. Kansas State University. Available online at http://fmso.leavenworth.army.mil/Collaboration/universities/Balochistan_final.pdf.

Heehs, P. 1988. *India's Freedom Struggle, a Short History*. Oxford University Press.

Hehir, A. 2010. *Humanitarian Intervention: An Introduction*. Red Globe Press.

Heintze, H. J. 1998. *Autonomy: Applications and Implications*. Edited by W. Suksi. Kluwer Law International.

Hodges, T. 1983. *Western Sahara: The Roots of a Desert War*. Lawrence Hill Books.

Hoof, G. J. 1983. *Rethinking the Sources of International Law*.

Hutchinson, J., and D. A. Smith. 1994. *Nationalism*. New York: Oxford University Press.

Islam, R. 1978. In *Language and Civilization Change in South Asia*. Edited by Maloney, C. E, T, Brill, Leiden. The Netherlands.

Jaffrelot, C. 2002. *Pakistan: Nationalism without a Nation*. London: Zed Books.

Jaffrelot, C. 2004. *A History of Pakistan and Its Origins*. Edited by C. Jaffrelot. London: Anthem Press.

Jayapalan, N. 2001. *History of India: Vol. I*. Atlantic Publishers.

Jensen, E. 2005. *Western Sahara: Anatomy of a Stalemate*. Lynne Rienner Publishers.

Johnson. D. H. 2003. *The Root Cause of Sudan's Civil Wars*. Kampala: Fountain Publishers.

Kiernan, B. 2008. *Genocide and Resistance in Southeast Asia: Documentation, Denial, and Justice in Cambodia and East Timor*. Transaction Publishers.

Kochler, H. 2001. *The Concept of Humanitarian Intervention in the Context of Modern Power Politics*. Vienna: International Progress Organization.

Kolb, R. 2013. *The International Court of Justice*. Bloomsbury Publishing.

Lapidoth, R. 1997. *Autonomy: Flexible Solutions to Ethnic Conflicts*. US Institute of Peace Press.

LaPorte, R. 1972. "Pakistan in 1971: The Disintegration of a Nation." *Asian Survey*.

Lissitzyn, O. J. 2006. *The International Court of Justice: Its Role in the Maintenance of International Peace and Security*. The Lawbook Exchange Ltd.

Locke, J. 1821. *Two Treaties of Government*. New edition printed in London.

Low, D. A. 1993. *Eclipse of Empire*. Cambridge and London: Cambridge University Press.

Marri, S. K. 2007. In *The Voice of Reason*. Edited by N. Dashti. Quetta: Asaap Publication.

Mayall, J. 2008. "Nationalism and Self-Determination." In *Settling Self-Determination Disputes: Complex Power-Sharing in the Theory and Practice*, edited by M. Weller and B. Metzger. Koninklijke Brill.

McCorquodale, R. 1996. "Human Rights and Self-Determination." In *The New World Order: Sovereignty, Human Rights, and the Self-Determination of Peoples*, edited by M. Sellers. Berg.

McGarr, P. M. 2013. *The Cold War in South Asia: Britain, the United States and the Indian Subcontinent, 1945–1965*. Cambridge University Press.

McWhinney, E. 2007. *Self-Determination of Peoples and the Plural-Ethnic States in Contemporary International Law: Failed States, Nation-Building and the Alternative, Federal Option*. Martinus Nijhoff Publishers.

Mill, J. 1817. *The History of British India, Vol. 1*. London: Baldwin and Cradock.

Murphy, D. S. 1996. *Humanitarian Intervention: The United Nations in an Evolving World Order*. University of Pennsylvania Press.

Murswiek, D. 1993. "The Issue of a Right of Secession." In *Modern Law of Self-Determination*, edited by C. Tomuschat. Martinus Nijhoff Publisher.

Naravane, M. S. 2007. *Battles of the Honourable East India Company.* APH Publishing Corporation.

Narayanan, M. S. 2006. *Calicut: The City of Truth*. Calicut University Publications.

Nyaba, P. A. 1997. *The Politics of Liberation in South Sudan: An Insider's View*. Fountain Publishers.

O'Malley, L. S. S., ICS. 1908. *Bankura Bengal District Gazetteers*. Published by Government of West Bengal.

Orford, A. 2003. *Reading Humanitarian Intervention: Human Rights and the Use of Force in International Law*. Cambridge Press.

Pakenham, T. 1991. *Scramble for Africa: The White Man's Conquest of the Dark Continent from 1876–1912*.

Pubantz, Jerry, and John Allphin Moore Jr. 2008. "Moscow Conference of Foreign Ministers." Modern World History (Second Ed.). New York: Facts on File.

Ray, B. 1998. *Balochistan and the Partition of India: The Forgotten Story*. Occasional Paper. New Delhi: South Asia Centre for Strategic Studies.

Ronen, Y. 2011. *Transition from Illegal Regimes under International Law, Self-Determination of Peoples: A Legal Reappraisal*. Cambridge: Cambridge University Press.

Siddiq, S. 1978. *Witness to Surrender*. Oxford University Press.

Sisson, R., and Leo E. Rose. 1990. *War and Secession: Pakistan, India, and the Creation of Bangladesh*. University of California Press.

Slomanson, William. 2011. *Fundamental Perspectives on International Law*. Boston, USA: Wadsworth.

Stiansen, E., and M. Kevane, eds. 1998. *Kordafan Invaded: Peripheral Incorporation and Social Transformation in Islamic Africa*. Boston: Brill Leiden.

Summers, J. 2007. *Peoples and International Law: How Nationalism and Self-Determination Shape a Contemporary Law of Nations.* Martinus Nijhoff Publishers.

Teny-Dhurgon, R. M. 1995. *South Sudan: A History of Political Domination—a Case of Self-Determination.* Available at http://www.africa.upenn.edu/Hornet/sd_machar.html.

Thirlway, H. W. A. 2016. *The International Court of Justice.* Oxford University Press.

UNMIS. 2004. Available at https://peacekeeping.un.org/en/mission/past/unmis/background.shtml.

Vattel, E. D. 1779. *The Law of Nations or the Principles of Natural Law Applied to the Conduct and to the Affairs of Nations and of Sovereigns.* New edition printed in London.

Vladimir Rudnitsky. 1996. *The New World Order: Sovereignty, Human Rights and the Self-Determination.* Edited by Martimer N. S. Sellers. Bloomsbury Publishing PLC.

Walter, Christian, A. V. Ungern- Sternberg, and K. Abushov, eds. *Self-Determination and Secession in International Law.* Oxford: Oxford University Press.

Weiss, G. T. 2012. *Humanitarian Intervention: Ideas in Action, 2nd Edition.* Polity Press.

Weller, M., and B. Metzger, eds. 2008. *Settling Self-Determination Disputes: Complex Power-Sharing in the Theory and Practice.* Koninklijke Brill.

Weller, M., and S. Wolff, eds. 2005. *Autonomy, Self-Governance and Conflict Resolution: Innovative Approaches to Institutional Design in Divided Societies.* Taylor & Francis.

Wellman, C. H. 2005. *A Theory of Secession: The Case for Political Self-Determination.* Cambridge University Press.

Zunes, S., and J. Mundy. 2010. *Western Sahara: War, Nationalism, and Conflict Irresolution.* Syracuse University Press.

INDEX

P

Pakistan, xi–xii, 3, 5, 9, 16–17, 25, 65, 99–105, 107, 109–10, 114, 116–29, 134, 137–41, 144–46, 149
Paris Convention, 48
Paris Peace Conference, 32, 77
Peace Plan, 96
Peace Treaty of Westphalia, 57
Persian Gulf, 110, 116
Perso-Baloch Boundary Commission, 113
Polisario, 91, 93–98
Portugal, 66, 70–71, 75, 88
Portuguese, 64, 66–72, 111
Pravda, 12
Puerto Rico, 40
Punjab, 100, 123

Q

Qajar dynasty, 113
Quetta, 116
Quit India movement, 115

R

Rabat, 96–98
Radi, Ali Mohammad Mussa, 81
Rahman, Mujibur (sheikh), 102, 123
Ramos-Horta, José, 74
Reza, Mohammad (king), 124
right of secession, 2, 6–7, 29, 36
Rind, 110
Roosevelt, Franklin D., 14, 60
Rudbar, 109
Russia, 111–13
Russian Empire, 29

S

Safavid dynasty, 110
Safi (shah), 110
Sahrawi, xviii, 5, 65, 90–98
Sahrawi Arab Democratic Republic, xviii, 93, 95
San Francisco Conference, 14, 60

Sanskrit, 99
Sarhad, 109
Sassanid Empire, 108
Saudi Arabia, 81
Scotland, 38
Scramble for Africa, 76, 88
Second World War, 1, 5, 11, 13–14, 17, 22, 27–28, 44, 55, 58, 60, 65, 67–68, 100, 105, 114–15, 131, 133, 143–44
Security Council, 52, 60–61, 70, 76, 93, 96–98, 132, 135–36
Selassie, Haile (emperor), 46, 77, 79–80
self-determination, v, xi–xii, 1–9, 11–15, 17–23, 25, 27–30, 32–39, 41–42, 45, 47, 49, 53–54, 59–60, 63–64, 70–71, 73–79, 81–83, 85, 88, 90–91, 93–94, 96–98, 105, 107, 118, 120, 123, 140–42, 145–49
self-government, 8, 15–16, 21, 39–41, 45, 47, 53–54, 96
Sena dynasty, 99
Sharia, 87
Sher Muhammad, 125
Sibi, 116
Sindh, 110, 123
Sindhis, 5, 17–18, 42, 104
Sindh River, 109
Singapore, 67
Siraj-ud-Daulah (nawab), 65
Sistan, 109
Six-Point Agenda, 102
Socialist Revolution, 12
South Sudan, 5, 8, 63–65, 83–86, 88–90, 105, 136, 149
sovereignty, 2, 5, 8, 17, 21, 23, 31–32, 37, 48–49, 57, 65, 77, 117, 132–33, 146, 148
Soviet Union, 12, 14, 35, 37–38, 51–52, 59–61, 78–79, 83, 116, 124, 134–35
Spain, 66, 88, 90–94
Stalin, Joseph, 11, 20, 60, 77

Sudan, 46, 64–65, 78, 81, 83–90, 105
Sudan African Nationalist Union, 85
Sudan People's Liberation Movement, 87–88
Suharto, 70–76
Suhrawardy, H. S., 101–3

T

Tamil, 17
Tehran, 16, 114
Timorese Democratic Union, xviii, 69
Timorese Popular Democratic Association, xvii, 69
Timorese Social Democratic Association, xvii, 69
Togoland, 82
Truman, 77
Turan, 109, 111
Turbat, 125
two-nation theory, 100, 116, 119

U

UNAMIS, xviii, 90
UN Charter, xii, 1, 15, 59, 70, 75, 141
Unionist Party, 81
United Kingdom, 20, 38, 59, 64, 105, 136, 139, 149
United Nations, xi, xviii–1, 3–8, 11, 13–15, 18, 20, 28–30, 32–33, 35–36, 43–46, 48, 53, 55, 59–65, 70–71, 73–83, 91, 93–95, 105–6, 131–32, 134–37, 141, 145, 148–49
United Nations Mission in East Timor, xviii, 76
United States, 28, 49, 51, 59–60, 70, 81, 94, 98, 105, 134–36, 139
Urdu, 102, 104
Usmani, Shabbir Ahmed, 101
USSR, 29, 59
Ustaman Gal, xviii, 121

V

Vienna Convention, 59–60

W

Washington, 52
Western Sahara, 8, 33–34, 63–65, 90–98
West Pakistan, 65, 100–102
West Timor, 66
Wilson, Woodrow, 11–13, 28, 32
Wolde-Michael, Asfaha, 81
World War I. *See* First World War
World War II. *See* Second World War

Y

Yemen, 81
Yugoslavia, 34–35, 37, 40, 43, 51, 135–36

Z

Zaranka, 109
Zia-ul-Haq (general), 124–25
Zoroastrian, 108